The Poetry of Lord Byron

The Poetry of Lord Byron

This edition published in 2020 by Arcturus Publishing Limited
26/27 Bickels Yard, 151–153 Bermondsey Street,
London SE1 3HA

AD007496UK

Printed in the UK

Contents

Introduction

On 22 January 1788, George Gordon Byron was born with a club foot in rented rooms on Oxford Street, London. When he died at 36, he was a literary legend, a national hero and arguably the first modern celebrity. He came from eccentric stock. His father was 'Mad Jack' Byron, a profligate captain of the Coldstream Guards with a penchant for marrying wealthier women and a remote relative of 'the Wicked Lord', Baron Byron. His mother, Catherine Gordon, was the captain's latest conquest. As an affluent Scottish heiress, she was an attractive prospect for 'Mad Jack', who had been cut off from his first wife's income after her death. By the time Byron was born, his father had managed to whittle away most of his new wife's wealth. He fled to France to escape his creditors, where he died in 1791.

Byron was unexpectedly elevated from a position of genteel poverty to one of aristocratic privilege when the heir to the barony was killed fighting in the French Revolutionary Wars, leaving Byron next in line. He inherited his great-uncle's title and estate upon his death in 1798.

He left Aberdeen Grammar School to attend Harrow in 1801 before moving on to Trinity College, Cambridge, in 1805. It was here that he printed his first collection of poems, *Fugitive Pieces*, in 1806, republished the following year as *Hours of Idleness*. This collection was harshly critiqued in the *Edinburgh Review*. Far from being discouraged, Byron responded by writing the blistering satire *English Bards and Scotch Reviewers*.

In 1808, he graduated from Cambridge, having amassed a great deal of debt, and departed for the continent to undertake a Grand Tour of Europe. He returned to England in 1811, a year marked by the deaths of his mother and his close friends Charles Skinner and John Edleston. The following year he published the first two Cantos of *Childe Harold's Pilgrimage*. It proved to be a life-altering event. As Byron wrote: 'I awoke one morning and found myself famous.'

Byron was suddenly propelled into the public eye. What followed was a series of scandals, liaisons and lovers. A notable affair was with Lady Caroline Lamb, wife of the future prime minister Lord Melbourne, who famously dubbed him 'mad, bad, and dangerous to know'. His intimate relationship with his half-sister, Augusta, was also the source of much speculation. In 1815 he married Anne Milbanke, with whom he had his only legitimate child, Ada Lovelace, a key figure in the history of computing. Only a year later, the couple separated. With rumours swirling, Byron left England, never to return.

In Europe, he met Percy and Mary Shelley. The three literary giants spent the 'wet, uncongenial summer' of 1816 together in Geneva. Incessant rain led Byron to suggest a ghost story writing contest that saw the creation of Byron's *Fragment of a Novel* and, most famously, Mary Shelley's *Frankenstein*. Afterwards, Byron continued to travel around Europe, writing and publishing works all the while and flinging himself enthusiastically into local affairs. He later became involved in the Greeks' fight for independence from the Ottoman Empire. After supplying them with funds, he joined Greek revolutionaries in Missolonghi. Here, he met a rather anti-climactic end, catching a fever from which he never recovered. He died on 19 April 1824.

A Fragment

When, to their airy hall, my fathers' voice
Shall call my spirit, joyful in their choice;
When, pois'd upon the gale, my form shall ride,
Or, dark in mist, descend the mountain's side;
Oh! may my shade behold no sculptur'd urns,
To mark the spot where earth to earth returns:
No lengthen'd scroll, no praise-encumber'd stone;
My epitaph shall be my name alone:
If that with honour fail to crown my clay,
Oh! may no other fame my deeds repay;
That, only that, shall single out the spot;
By that remember'd, or with that forgot.

On Leaving Newstead Abbey

*Why dost thou build the hall, Son of the winged days? Thou lookest from
thy tower today: yet a few years, and the blast of the desert comes: it howls
in thy empty court.*

  —Ossian.

I

Through thy battlements, Newstead, the hollow winds
  whistle:
  Thou, the hall of my Fathers, art gone to decay;
In thy once smiling garden, the hemlock and thistle
   Have choak'd up the rose, which late bloom'd in
    the way.

II

Of the mail-cover'd Barons, who, proudly, to battle,
  Led their vassals from Europe to Palestine's plain,
The escutcheon and shield, which with ev'ry blast rattle,
   Are the only sad vestiges now that remain.

III

No more doth old Robert, with harp-stringing numbers,
   Raise a flame, in the breast, for the war-laurell'd
    wreath;
Near Askalon's towers, John of Horistan slumbers,
   Unnerv'd is the hand of his minstrel, by death.

IV

Paul and Hubert too sleep in the valley of Cressy;
   For the safety of Edward and England they fell:

My Fathers! the tears of your country redress ye:
　　How you fought! how you died! still her annals can
　　　　tell.

V

On Marston, with Rupert, 'gainst traitors contending,
　　Four brothers enrich'd, with their blood, the bleak
　　　　field;
For the rights of a monarch their country defending,
　　Till death their attachment to royalty seal'd.

VI

Shades of heroes, farewell! your descendant departing
　　From the seat of his ancestors, bids you adieu!
Abroad, or at home, your remembrance imparting
　　New courage, he'll think upon glory and you.

VII

Though a tear dim his eye at this sad separation,
　　'Tis nature, not fear, that excites his regret;
Far distant he goes, with the same emulation,
　　The fame of his Fathers he ne'er can forget.

VIII

That fame, and that memory, still will he cherish;
　　He vows that he ne'er will disgrace your renown:
Like you will he live, or like you will he perish;
　　When decay'd, may he mingle his dust with
　　　　your own!

To Caroline I, II, III & IV

To Caroline I

I

Think'st thou I saw thy beauteous eyes,
  Suffus'd in tears, implore to stay;
And heard unmov'd thy plenteous sighs,
  Which said far more than words can say?

II

Though keen the grief thy tears exprest,
  When love and hope lay both o'erthrown;
Yet still, my girl, this bleeding breast
  Throbb'd, with deep sorrow, as thine own.

III

But, when our cheeks with anguish glow'd,
  When thy sweet lips were join'd to mine;
The tears that from my eyelids flow'd
  Were lost in those which fell from thine.

IV

Thou could'st not feel my burning cheek,
  Thy gushing tears had quench'd its flame,
And, as thy tongue essay'd to speak,
  In sighs alone it breath'd my name.

V

And yet, my girl, we weep in vain,
  In vain our fate in sighs deplore;

Remembrance only can remain,
> But *that* will make us weep the more.

VI

Again, thou best belov'd, adieu!
> Ah! if thou canst, o'ercome regret,

Nor let thy mind past joys review,
> Our only *hope* is, to *forget!*

To Caroline II

I

You say you love, and yet your eye
> No symptom of that love conveys,

You say you love, yet know not why,
> Your cheek no sign of love betrays.

II

Ah! did that breast with ardour glow,
With me alone it joy could know,
Or feel with me the listless woe,
> Which racks my heart when far from thee.

III

Whene'er we meet my blushes rise,
> And mantle through my purpled cheek,

But yet no blush to mine replies,
> Nor e'en your eyes your love bespeak.

IV

Your voice alone declares your flame,
And though so sweet it breathes my name,

Our passions still are not the same;
    Alas! you cannot love like me.

V

For e'en your lip seems steep'd in snow,
    And though so oft it meets my kiss,
It burns with no responsive glow,
    Nor melts like mine in dewy bliss.

VI

Ah! what are words to love like *mine*
Though uttered by a voice like thine,
I still in murmurs must repine,
    And think that love can ne'er be *true*,

VII

Which meets me with no joyous sign,
    Without a sigh which bids adieu;
How different is my love from thine,
    How keen my grief when leaving you.

VIII

Your image fills my anxious breast,
Till day declines adown the West,
And when at night, I sink to rest,
    In dreams your fancied form I view.

IX

'Tis then your breast, no longer cold,
    With equal ardour seems to burn,
While close your arms around me fold,
    Your lips my kiss with warmth return.

X

Ah! would these joyous moments last;
Vain HOPE! the gay delusion's past,
That voice! – ah! no, 'tis but the blast,
    Which echoes through the neighbouring grove.

XI

But when *awake*, your lips I seek,
    And clasp enraptur'd all your charms,
So chill's the pressure of your cheek,
    I fold a statue in my arms.

XII

If thus, when to my heart embrac'd,
No pleasure in your eyes is trac'd,
You may be prudent, fair, and *chaste*,
    But ah! my girl, you *do not love*.

To Caroline III

I

Oh! when shall the grave hide for ever my sorrow?
    Oh! when shall my soul wing her flight from this
        clay?
The present is hell! and the coming tomorrow
    But brings, with new torture, the curse of today.

II

From my eye flows no tear, from my lips flow no curses,
    I blast not the fiends who have hurl'd me from bliss;
For poor is the soul which, bewailing, rehearses
    Its querulous grief, when in anguish like this –

III

Was my eye, 'stead of tears, with red fury flakes bright'ning,
> Would my lips breathe a flame which no stream
> > could assuage,
On our foes should my glance launch in vengeance its lightning,
> With transport my tongue give a loose to its rage.

IV

But now tears and curses, alike unavailing,
> Would add to the souls of our tyrants delight;
Could they view us our sad separation bewailing,
> Their merciless hearts would rejoice at the sight.

V

Yet, still, though we bend with a feign'd resignation,
> Life beams not for us with one ray that can cheer;
Love and Hope upon earth bring no more consolation,
> In the grave is our hope, for in life is our fear.

VI

Oh! when, my ador'd, in the tomb will they place me,
> Since, in life, love and friendship for ever are fled?
If again in the mansion of death I embrace thee,
> Perhaps they will leave unmolested – the dead.

To Caroline IV

I

When I hear you express an affection so warm,
> Ne'er think, my belov'd, that I do not believe;

For your lip would the soul of suspicion disarm,
    And your eye beams a ray which can never deceive.

II

Yet still, this fond bosom regrets, while adoring,
    That love, like the leaf, must fall into the sear;
That Age will come on, when Remembrance, deploring,
    Contemplates the scenes of her youth, with a tear;

III

That the time must arrive, when, no longer retaining
    Their auburn, those locks must wave thin to the
        breeze;
When a few silver hairs of those tresses remaining,
    Prove nature a prey to decay and disease.

IV

'Tis this, my belov'd, which spreads gloom o'er my
    features,
    Though I ne'er shall presume to arraign the decree,
Which God has proclaim'd as the fate of his creatures,
    In the death which one day will deprive you of me.

V

Mistake not, sweet sceptic, the cause of emotion,
    No doubt can the mind of your lover invade;
He worships each look with such faithful devotion,
    A smile can enchant, or a tear can dissuade.

VI

But as death, my belov'd, soon or late shall o'ertake us,
    And our breasts, which alive with such sympathy glow,

Will sleep in the grave, till the blast shall awake us,
    When calling the dead, in Earth's bosom laid low.

VII

Oh! then let us drain, while we may, draughts of pleasure,
    Which from passion, like ours, must unceasingly
        flow;
Let us pass round the cup of Love's bliss in full measure,
    And quaff the contents as our nectar below.

To Woman

Woman! experience might have told me
That all must love thee, who behold thee:
Surely experience might have taught
Thy firmest promises are nought;
But, plac'd in all thy charms before me,
All I forget, but to *adore* thee.
Oh memory! thou choicest blessing,
When join'd with hope, when still possessing;
But how much curst by every lover
When hope is fled, and passion's over.
Woman, that fair and fond deceiver,
How prompt are striplings to believe her!
How throbs the pulse, when first we view
The eye that rolls in glossy blue,
Or sparkles black, or mildly throws
A beam from under hazel brows!
How quick we credit every oath,
And hear her plight the willing troth!
Fondly we hope 'twill last for ay,
When, lo! she changes in a day.
This record will for ever stand,
'Woman, thy vows are trac'd in sand.'

The Cornelian

I

No specious splendour of this stone
    Endears it to my memory ever;
With lustre *only once* it shone,
    And blushes modest as the giver.

II

Some, who can sneer at friendship's ties,
    Have, for my weakness, oft reprov'd me;
Yet still the simple gift I prize,
    For I am sure, the giver lov'd me.

III

He offer'd it with downcast look,
    As *fearful* that I might refuse it;
I told him, when the gift I took,
    My *only fear* should be, to lose it.

IV

This pledge attentively I view'd,
    And *sparkling* as I held it near,
Methought one drop the stone bedew'd,
    And, ever since, *I've lov'd a tear.*

V

Still, to adorn his humble youth,
    Nor wealth nor birth their treasures yield;
But he, who seeks the flowers of truth,
    Must quit the garden, for the field.

VI

'Tis not the plant uprear'd in sloth,
    Which beauty shews, and sheds perfume;
The flowers, which yield the most of both,
    In Nature's wild luxuriance bloom.

VII

Had Fortune aided Nature's care,
    For once forgetting to be blind,
His would have been an ample share,
    If well proportioned to his mind.

VIII

But had the Goddess clearly seen,
    His form had fix'd her fickle breast;
Her countless hoards would his have been,
    And none remain'd to give the rest.

I Would I Were a Careless Child

I

I would I were a careless child,
    Still dwelling in my Highland cave,
Or roaming through the dusky wild,
    Or bounding o'er the dark blue wave;
The cumbrous pomp of Saxon pride,
    Accords not with the freeborn soul,
Which loves the mountain's craggy side,
    And seeks the rocks where billows roll.

II

Fortune! take back these cultur'd lands,
    Take back this name of splendid sound!
I hate the touch of servile hands,
    I hate the slaves that cringe around:
Place me among the rocks I love,
    Which sound to Ocean's wildest roar;
I ask but this – again to rove
    Through scenes my youth hath known before.

III

Few are my years, and yet I feel
    The World was ne'er design'd for me:
Ah! why do dark'ning shades conceal
    The hour when man must cease to be?
Once I beheld a splendid dream,
    A visionary scene of bliss:
Truth! – wherefore did thy hated beam
    Awake me to a world like this?

IV

I lov'd – but those I lov'd are gone;
　　Had friends – my early friends are fled:
How cheerless feels the heart alone,
　　When all its former hopes are dead!
Though gay companions, o'er the bowl
　　Dispel awhile the sense of ill;
Though Pleasure stirs the maddening soul,
　　The heart – the heart – is lonely still.

V

How dull! to hear the voice of those
　　Whom Rank or Chance, whom Wealth or Power,
Have made, though neither friends nor foes,
　　Associates of the festive hour.
Give me again a faithful few,
　　In years and feelings still the same,
And I will fly the midnight crew,
　　Where boist'rous Joy is but a name.

VI

And Woman, lovely Woman! thou,
　　My hope, my comforter, my all!
How cold must be my bosom now,
　　When e'en thy smiles begin to pall!
Without a sigh would I resign,
　　This busy scene of splendid Woe,
To make that calm contentment mine,
　　Which Virtue knows, or seems to know.

VII

Fain would I fly the haunts of men –
    I seek to shun, not hate mankind;
My breast requires the sullen glen,
    Whose gloom may suit a darken'd mind.
Oh! that to me the wings were given,
    Which bear the turtle to her nest!
Then would I cleave the vault of Heaven,
    To flee away, and be at rest.

Lachin Y Gair

I

Away, ye gay landscapes, ye gardens of roses!
　　In you let the minions of luxury rove;
Restore me the rocks, where the snow-flake reposes,
　　Though still they are sacred to freedom and love:
Yet, Caledonia, belov'd are thy mountains,
　　Round their white summits though elements war;
Though cataracts foam 'stead of smooth-flowing fountains,
　　I sigh for the valley of dark Loch na Garr.

II

Ah! there my young footsteps in infancy, wander'd:
　　My cap was the bonnet, my cloak was the plaid;
On chieftains, long perish'd, my memory ponder'd,
　　As daily I strode through the pine-cover'd glade;
I sought not my home, till the day's dying glory
　　Gave place to the rays of the bright polar star;
For fancy was cheer'd, by traditional story,
　　Disclos'd by the natives of dark Loch na Garr.

III

'Shades of the dead! have I not heard your voices
　　Rise on the night-rolling breath of the gale?'
Surely, the soul of the hero rejoices,
　　And rides on the wind, o'er his own Highland vale!
Round Loch na Garr, while the stormy mist gathers,
　　Winter presides in his cold icy car:
Clouds, there, encircle the forms of my Fathers;
　　They dwell in the tempests of dark Loch na Garr.

IV

'Ill starr'd, though brave, did no visions foreboding
    Tell you that fate had forsaken your cause?'
Ah! were you destined to die at Culloden,
    Victory crown'd not your fall with applause:
Still were you happy, in death's earthy slumber,
    You rest with your clan, in the caves of Braemar;
The Pibroch resounds, to the piper's loud number,
    Your deeds, on the echoes of dark Loch na Garr.

V

Years have roll'd on, Loch na Garr, since I left you,
    Years must elapse, ere I tread you again:
Nature of verdure and flowers has bereft you,
    Yet still are you dearer than Albion's plain:
England! thy beauties are tame and domestic,
    To one who has rov'd on the mountains afar:
Oh! for the crags that are wild and majestic,
    The steep, frowning glories of dark Loch na Garr.

Damætas

In law an infant, and in years a boy,
In mind a slave to every vicious joy;
From every sense of shame and virtue wean'd,
In lies an adept, in deceit a fiend;
Vers'd in hypocrisy, while yet a child;
Fickle as wind, of inclinations wild;
Woman his dupe, his heedless friend a tool;
Old in the world, though scarcely broke from school;
Damætas ran through all the maze of sin,
And found the goal, when others just begin:
Ev'n still conflicting passions shake his soul,
And bid him drain the dregs of Pleasure's bowl;
But, pall'd with vice, he breaks his former chain,
And what was once his bliss appears his bane.

To a Lady, On Being Asked My Reason for Quitting England in the Spring

I

When Man, expell'd from Eden's bowers,
    A moment linger'd near the gate,
Each scene recall'd the vanish'd hours,
    And bade him curse his future fate.

II

But, wandering on through distant climes,
    He learnt to bear his load of grief;
Just gave a sigh to other times,
    And found in busier scenes relief.

III

Thus, Lady! will it be with me,
    And I must view thy charms no more;
For, while I linger near to thee,
    I sigh for all I knew before.

IV

In flight I shall be surely wise,
    Escaping from temptation's snare;
I cannot view my Paradise
    Without the wish of dwelling there.

Lines Inscribed Upon a Cup Formed from a Skull

I

Start not – nor deem my spirit fled:
    In me behold the only skull,
From which, unlike a living head,
    Whatever flows is never dull.

II

I lived, I loved, I quaff'd, like thee:
    I died: let earth my bones resign;
Fill up – thou canst not injure me;
    The worm hath fouler lips than thine.

III

Better to hold the sparkling grape,
    Than nurse the earth-worm's slimy brood;
And circle in the goblet's shape
    The drink of Gods, than reptile's food.

IV

Where once my wit, perchance, hath shone,
    In aid of others' let me shine;
And when, alas! our brains are gone,
    What nobler substitute than wine?

V

Quaff while thou canst: another race,
    When thou and thine, like me, are sped,
May rescue thee from earth's embrace,
    And rhyme and revel with the dead.

VI

Why not? since through life's little day
    Our heads such sad effects produce;
Redeem'd from worms and wasting clay,
    This chance is theirs, to be of use.

Well! Thou Art Happy

I

Well! thou art happy, and I feel
    That I should thus be happy too;
For still my heart regards thy weal
    Warmly, as it was wont to do.

II

Thy husband's blest – and 'twill impart
    Some pangs to view his happier lot:
But let them pass – Oh! how my heart
    Would hate him, if he loved thee not!

III

When late I saw thy favourite child,
    I thought my jealous heart would break;
But when the unconscious infant smil'd,
    I kiss'd it for its mother's sake.

IV

I kiss'd it, – and repress'd my sighs
    Its father in its face to see;
But then it had its mother's eyes,
    And they were all to love and me.

V

Mary, adieu! I must away:
    While thou art blest I'll not repine;
But near thee I can never stay;
    My heart would soon again be thine.

VI

I deem'd that time, I deem'd that pride
    Had quench'd at length my boyish flame;
Nor knew, till seated by thy side,
    My heart in all, – save hope, – the same.

VII

Yet was I calm: I knew the time
    My breast would thrill before thy look;
But now to tremble were a crime –
    We met, – and not a nerve was shook.

VIII

I saw thee gaze upon my face,
    Yet met with no confusion there:
One only feeling could'st thou trace;
    The sullen calmness of despair.

IX

Away! away! my early dream
    Remembrance never must awake:
Oh! where is Lethe's fabled stream?
    My foolish heart be still, or break.

When We Two Parted

When we two parted
    In silence and tears,
Half broken-hearted
    To sever for years,
Pale grew thy cheek and cold,
    Colder thy kiss;
Truly that hour foretold
    Sorrow to this.

The dew of the morning
    Sunk chill on my brow –
It felt like the warning
    Of what I feel now.
Thy vows are all broken,
    And light is thy fame:
I hear thy name spoken,   → awwn
    And share in its shame.

They name thee before me,
    A knell to mine ear;
A shudder comes o'er me –
    Why wert thou so dear?
They know not I knew thee,
    Who knew thee too well: –
Long, long shall I rue thee,
    Too deeply to tell.

In secret we met –
    In silence I grieve,   → almost like for older lovers
That thy heart could forget,

Thy spirit deceive.
If I should meet thee
    After long years,
How should I greet thee? –
    With silence and tears.

Stanzas Composed During a Thunderstorm

I

Chill and mirk is the nightly blast,
    Where Pindus' mountains rise,
And angry clouds are pouring fast
    The vengeance of the skies.

II

Our guides are gone, our hope is lost,
    And lightnings, as they play,
But show where rocks our path have crost,
    Or gild the torrent's spray.

III

Is yon a cot I saw, though low?
    When lightning broke the gloom –
How welcome were its shade! – ah, no!
    'Tis but a Turkish tomb.

IV

Through sounds of foaming waterfalls,
    I hear a voice exclaim –
My way-worn countryman, who calls
    On distant England's name.

V

A shot is fired – by foe or friend?
    Another – 'tis to tell
The mountain-peasants to descend,
    And lead us where they dwell.

VI

Oh! who in such a night will dare
    To tempt the wilderness?
And who 'mid thunder-peals can hear
    Our signal of distress?

VII

And who that heard our shouts would rise
    To try the dubious road?
Nor rather deem from nightly cries
    That outlaws were abroad.

VIII

Clouds burst, skies flash, oh, dreadful hour!
    More fiercely pours the storm!
Yet here one thought has still the power
    To keep my bosom warm.

IX

While wandering through each broken path,
    O'er brake and craggy brow;
While elements exhaust their wrath,
    Sweet Florence, where art thou?

X

Not on the sea, not on the sea –
    Thy bark hath long been gone:
Oh, may the storm that pours on me,
    Bow down my head alone!

XI

Full swiftly blew the swift Siroc,
    When last I press'd thy lip;
And long ere now, with foaming shock,
    Impelled thy gallant ship.

XII

Now thou art safe; nay, long ere now
    Hast trod the shore of Spain;
'Twere hard if aught so fair as thou
    Should linger on the main.

XIII

And since I now remember thee
    In darkness and in dread,
As in those hours of revelry
    Which Mirth and Music sped;

XIV

Do thou, amid the fair white walls,
    If Cadiz yet be free,
At times from out her latticed halls
    Look o'er the dark blue sea;

XV

Then think upon Calypso's isles,
    Endeared by days gone by;
To others give a thousand smiles,
    To me a single sigh.

XVI

And when the admiring circle mark
    The paleness of thy face,
A half-formed tear, a transient spark
    Of melancholy grace,

XVII

Again thou'lt smile, and blushing shun
    Some coxcomb's raillery;
Nor own for once thou thought'st on one,
    Who ever thinks on thee.

XVIII

Though smile and sigh alike are vain,
    When severed hearts repine,
My spirit flies o'er Mount and Main,
    And mourns in search of thine.

Lines to Mr Hodgson

Written on Board the Lisbon Packet.

I

Huzza! Hodgson, we are going,
    Our embargo's off at last;
Favourable breezes blowing
    Bend the canvas o'er the mast.
From aloft the signal's streaming,
    Hark! the farewell gun is fired;
Women screeching, tars blaspheming,
    Tell us that our time's expired.
        Here's a rascal
        Come to task all,
Prying from the Custom-house;
        Trunks unpacking
        Cases cracking,
    Not a corner for a mouse
'Scapes unsearched amid the racket,
Ere we sail on board the Packet.

II

Now our boatmen quit their mooring,
    And all hands must ply the oar;
Baggage from the quay is lowering,
    We're impatient, push from shore.
'Have a care! that case holds liquor –
    Stop the boat – I'm sick – oh Lord!'
'Sick, Ma'am, damme, you'll be sicker,
    Ere you've been an hour on board.'
        Thus are screaming

          Men and women,
       Gemmen, ladies, servants, Jacks;
          Here entangling,
          All are wrangling,
       Stuck together close as wax. —
Such the general noise and racket,
Ere we reach the Lisbon Packet.

                    III

Now we've reached her, lo! the Captain,
       Gallant Kidd, commands the crew;
Passengers their berths are clapt in,
       Some to grumble, some to spew.
'Hey day! call you that a cabin?
       Why 'tis hardly three feet square:
Not enough to stow Queen Mab in —
       Who the deuce can harbour there?'
          'Who, sir? plenty —
          Nobles twenty
       Did at once my vessel fill.' —
          'Did they? Jesus,
          How you squeeze us!
       Would to God they did so still:
Then I'd 'scape the heat and racket
Of the good ship, Lisbon Packet.'

                    IV

Fletcher! Murray! Bob! where are you?
       Stretched along the deck like logs —
Bear a hand, you jolly tar, you!
       Here's a rope's end for the dogs.
Hobhouse muttering fearful curses,

As the hatchway down he rolls,
Now his breakfast, now his verses,
   Vomits forth — and damns our souls.
      'Here's a stanza
      On Braganza —
   Help!' — 'A couplet?' — 'No, a cup
      Of warm water—'
      'What's the matter?'
   'Zounds! my liver's coming up;
I shall not survive the racket
Of this brutal Lisbon Packet.'

                        V

Now at length we're off for Turkey,
   Lord knows when we shall come back!
Breezes foul and tempests murky
   May unship us in a crack.
But, since Life at most a jest is,
   As philosophers allow,
Still to laugh by far the best is,
   Then laugh on — as I do now.
      Laugh at all things,
      Great and small things,
   Sick or well, at sea or shore;
      While we're quaffing,
      Let's have laughing —
   Who the devil cares for more? —
Some good wine! and who would lack it,
Ev'n on board the Lisbon Packet?

Maid of Athens, Ere We Part

Ζωή μου, σᾶς ἀγαπῶ.

I

Maid of Athens, ere we part,
Give, oh, give me back my heart!
Or, since that has left my breast,
Keep it now, and take the rest!
Hear my vow before I go,
Ζωή μου, σᾶς ἀγαπῶ.

II

By those tresses unconfined,
Wooed by each Ægean wind;
By those lids whose jetty fringe
Kiss thy soft cheeks' blooming tinge;
By those wild eyes like the roe,
Ζωή μου, σᾶς ἀγαπῶ.

III

By that lip I long to taste;
By that zone-encircled waist;
By all the token-flowers that tell
What words can never speak so well;
By love's alternate joy and woe,
Ζωή μου, σᾶς ἀγαπῶ.

IV

Maid of Athens! I am gone:
Think of me, sweet! when alone.
Though I fly to Istambol,

Athens holds my heart and soul:
Can I cease to love thee? No!
Ζωή μου, σᾶς ἀγαπῶ.

Written after Swimming from Sestos to Abydos

I

If, in the month of dark December,
    Leander, who was nightly wont
(What maid will not the tale remember?)
    To cross thy stream, broad Hellespont!

II

If, when the wintry tempest roared,
    He sped to Hero, nothing loth,
And thus of old thy current poured,
    Fair Venus! how I pity both!

III

For me, degenerate modern wretch,
    Though in the genial month of May,
My dripping limbs I faintly stretch,
    And think I've done a feat today.

IV

But since he crossed the rapid tide,
    According to the doubtful story,
To woo, – and – Lord knows what beside,
    And swam for Love, as I for Glory;

V

'Twere hard to say who fared the best:
    Sad mortals! thus the Gods still plague you!
He lost his labour, I my jest:
    For he was drowned, and I've the ague.

Epistle to a Friend

In Answer to Some Lines Exhorting the Author to Be Cheerful, and to 'Banish Care.'

'Oh! banish care' – such ever be
The motto of thy revelry!
Perchance of mine, when wassail nights
Renew those riotous delights,
Wherewith the children of Despair
Lull the lone heart, and 'banish care'.
But not in Morn's reflecting hour,
When present, past, and future lower,
When all I loved is changed or gone,
Mock with such taunts the woes of one,
Whose every thought – but let them pass –
Thou know'st I am not what I was.
But, above all, if thou wouldst hold
Place in a heart that ne'er was cold,
By all the powers that men revere,
By all unto thy bosom dear,
Thy joys below, thy hopes above,
Speak – speak of anything but Love.

'Twere long to tell, and vain to hear,
The tale of one who scorns a tear;
And there is little in that tale
Which better bosoms would bewail.
But mine has suffered more than well
'Twould suit philosophy to tell.
I've seen my bride another's bride, –
Have seen her seated by his side, –

Have seen the infant, which she bore,
Wear the sweet smile the mother wore,
When she and I in youth have smiled,
As fond and faultless as her child; –
Have seen her eyes, in cold disdain,
Ask if I felt no secret pain;
And I have acted well my part,
And made my cheek belie my heart,
Returned the freezing glance she gave,
Yet felt the while that woman's slave; –
Have kissed, as if without design,
The babe which ought to have been mine,
And showed, alas! in each caress,
Time had not made me love the less.

But let this pass – I'll whine no more,
Nor seek again an eastern shore;
The world befits a busy brain, –
I'll hie me to its haunts again.
But if, in some succeeding year,
When Britain's 'May is in the sere',
Thou hear'st of one, whose deepening crimes
Suit with the sablest of the times,
Of one, whom love nor pity sways,
Nor hope of fame, nor good men's praise;
One, who in stern Ambition's pride,
Perchance not blood shall turn aside;
One ranked in some recording page
With the worst anarchs of the age,
Him wilt thou know – and knowing pause,
Nor with the effect forget the cause.

Lines Written Beneath a Picture

I

Dear object of defeated care!
    Though now of Love and thee bereft,
To reconcile me with despair
    Thine image and my tears are left.

II

'Tis said with Sorrow Time can cope;
    But this I feel can ne'er be true:
For by the death-blow of my Hope
    My Memory immortal grew.

To Thyrza

Without a stone to mark the spot,
    And say, what Truth might well have said,
By all, save one, perchance forgot,
    Ah! wherefore art thou lowly laid?
By many a shore and many a sea
    Divided, yet beloved in vain;
The Past, the Future fled to thee,
    To bid us meet – no – ne'er again!
Could this have been – a word, a look,
    That softly said, 'We part in peace',
Had taught my bosom how to brook,
    With fainter sighs, thy soul's release.
And didst thou not, since Death for thee
    Prepared a light and pangless dart,
Once long for him thou ne'er shalt see,
    Who held, and holds thee in his heart?
Oh! who like him had watched thee here?
    Or sadly marked thy glazing eye,
In that dread hour ere Death appear,
    When silent Sorrow fears to sigh,
Till all was past? But when no more
    'Twas thine to reck of human woe,
Affection's heart-drops, gushing o'er,
    Had flowed as fast – as now they flow.
Shall they not flow, when many a day
    In these, to me, deserted towers,
Ere called but for a time away,
    Affection's mingling tears were ours?
Ours too the glance none saw beside;
    The smile none else might understand;

The whispered thought of hearts allied,
　　The pressure of the thrilling hand;
The kiss, so guiltless and refined,
　　That Love each warmer wish forbore;
Those eyes proclaimed so pure a mind,
　　Ev'n Passion blushed to plead for more.
The tone, that taught me to rejoice,
　　When prone, unlike thee, to repine;
The song, celestial from thy voice,
　　But sweet to me from none but thine;
The pledge we wore – I wear it still,
　　But where is thine? – Ah! where art thou?
Oft have I borne the weight of ill,
　　But never bent beneath till now!
Well hast thou left in Life's best bloom
　　The cup of Woe for me to drain.
If rest alone be in the tomb,
　　I would not wish thee here again:
But if in worlds more blest than this
　　Thy virtues seek a fitter sphere,
Impart some portion of thy bliss,
　　To wean me from mine anguish here.
Teach me – too early taught by thee!
　　To bear, forgiving and forgiven:
On earth thy love was such to me;
　　It fain would form my hope in Heaven!

Childe Harold's Departure (from *Childe Harold's Pilgrimage*, Canto I)

Childe Harold bask'd him in the noon-tide sun,
Disporting there like any other fly;
Nor deem'd before his little day was done
One blast might chill him into misery.
But long ere scarce a third of his pass'd by,
Worse than adversity the Childe befell;
He felt the fulness of satiety:
Then loath'd he in his native land to dwell,
Which seem'd to him more lone than Eremite's sad cell.

For he through Sin's long labyrinth had run,
Nor made atonement when he did amiss,
Had sigh'd to many though he lov'd but one,
And that lov'd one, alas! could ne'er be his.
Ah, happy she! to 'scape from him whose kiss
Had been pollution unto aught so chaste;
Who soon had left her charms for vulgar bliss,
And spoil'd her goodly lands to gild his waste,
Nor calm domestic peace had ever deign'd to taste.

And now Childe Harold was sore sick at heart,
And from his fellow bacchanals would flee;
'Tis said, at times the sullen tear would start,
But Pride congeal'd the drop within his ee:
Apart he stalk'd in joyless reverie,
And from his native land resolv'd to go,
And visit scorching climes beyond the sea;
With pleasure drugg'd, he almost long'd for woe,
And e'en for change of scene would seek the shades below.

The Childe departed from his father's hall:
It was a vast and venerable pile;
So old, it seemed only not to fall,
Yet strength was pillar'd in each massy aisle.
Monastic dome! condemn'd to uses vile!
Where Superstition once had made her den
Now Paphian girls were known to sing and smile;
And monks might deem their time was come agen,
If ancient tales say true, nor wrong these holy men.

Yet oft-times in his maddest mirthful mood
Strange pangs would flash along Childe Harold's
      brow,
As if the memory of some deadly feud
Or disappointed passion lurk'd below:
But this none knew, nor haply car'd to know;
For his was not that open, artless soul
That feels relief by bidding sorrow flow,
Nor sought he friend to counsel or condole,
Whate'er this grief mote be, which he could not control.

And none did love him – though to hall and bower
He gather'd revellers from far and near,
He knew them flatt'rers of the festal hour;
The heartless parasites of present cheer.
Yea! none did love him – not his lemans dear –
But pomp and power alone are woman's care,
And where these are light Eros finds a feere;
Maidens, like moths, are ever caught by glare,
And Mammon wins his ways where Seraphs might
      despair.

Childe Harold had a mother – not forgot,
Though parting from that mother he did shun;
A sister whom he lov'd, but saw her not
Before his weary pilgrimage begun:
If friends he had, he bade adieu to none.
Yet deem not thence his breast a breast of steel;
Ye, who have known what 'tis to dote upon
A few dear objects, will in sadness feel
Such partings break the heart they fondly hope to heal.

His house, his home, his heritage, his lands,
The laughing dames in whom he did delight,
Whose large blue eyes, fair locks, and snowy hands
Might shake the saintship of an anchorite,
And long had fed his youthful appetite;
His goblets brimm'd with every costly wine,
And all that mote to luxury invite,
Without a sigh he left, to cross the brine,
And traverse Paynim shores, and pass Earth's central line.

One Struggle More, and I Am Free

One struggle more, and I am free
    From pangs that rend my heart in twain;
One last long sigh to Love and thee,
    Then back to busy life again.
It suits me well to mingle now
    With things that never pleased before:
Though every joy is fled below,
    What future grief can touch me more?

Then bring me wine, the banquet bring;
    Man was not formed to live alone: *and yet someho*
I'll be that light unmeaning thing
    That smiles with all, and weeps with none.
It was not thus in days more dear,
    It never would have been, but thou
Hast fled, and left me lonely here;
    Thou'rt nothing, – all are nothing now.

In vain my lyre would lightly breathe!
    The smile that Sorrow fain would wear
But mocks the woe that lurks beneath,
    Like roses o'er a sepulchre.
Though gay companions o'er the bowl
    Dispel awhile the sense of ill;
Though Pleasure fires the maddening soul,
    The Heart, – the Heart is lonely still!

On many a lone and lovely night
    It soothed to gaze upon the sky;
For then I deemed the heavenly light

Shone sweetly on thy pensive eye:
And oft I thought at Cynthia's noon,
When sailing o'er the Ægean wave,
'Now Thyrza gazes on that moon –'
Alas, it gleamed upon her grave!

When stretched on fever's sleepless bed,
And sickness shrunk my throbbing veins,
''Tis comfort still,' I faintly said,
'That Thyrza cannot know my pains:'
Like freedom to the time-worn slave –
A boon 'tis idle then to give –
Relenting Nature vainly gave
My life, when Thyrza ceased to live!

My Thyrza's pledge in better days,
When Love and Life alike were new!
How different now thou meet'st my gaze!
How tinged by time with Sorrow's hue!
The heart that gave itself with thee
Is silent – ah, were mine as still!
Though cold as e'en the dead can be,
It feels, it sickens with the chill.

Thou bitter pledge! thou mournful token!
Though painful, welcome to my breast!
Still, still, preserve that love unbroken,
Or break the heart to which thou'rt pressed!
Time tempers Love, but not removes,
More hallowed when its Hope is fled:
Oh! what are thousand living loves
To that which cannot quit the dead?

Euthanasia

When Time, or soon or late, shall bring
    The dreamless sleep that lulls the dead,
Oblivion! may thy languid wing
    Wave gently o'er my dying bed!

No band of friends or heirs be there,
    To weep, or wish, the coming blow:
No maiden, with dishevelled hair,
    To feel, or feign, decorous woe.

But silent let me sink to Earth,
    With no officious mourners near:
I would not mar one hour of mirth,
    Nor startle Friendship with a fear.

Yet Love, if Love in such an hour
    Could nobly check its useless sighs,
Might then exert its latest power
    In her who lives and him who dies.

'Twere sweet, my Psyche! to the last
    Thy features still serene to see:
Forgetful of its struggles past,
    E'en Pain itself should smile on thee.

But vain the wish – for Beauty still
    Will shrink, as shrinks the ebbing breath;
And Woman's tears, produced at will,
    Deceive in life, unman in death.

Then lonely be my latest hour,
        Without regret, without a groan;
For thousands Death hath ceased to lower,
        And pain been transient or unknown.

'Ay, but to die, and go,' alas!
        Where all have gone, and all must go!
To be the nothing that I was
        Ere born to life and living woe!

Count o'er the joys thine hours have seen,
        Count o'er thy days from anguish free,
And know, whatever thou hast been,
        'Tis something better not to be.

Solitude (from *Childe Harold's Pilgrimage*, Canto II)

To sit on rocks – to muse o'er flood and fell –
To slowly trace the forest's shady scene,
Where things that own not Man's dominion dwell,
And mortal foot hath ne'er or rarely been;
To climb the trackless mountain all unseen.
With the wild flock that never needs a fold:
Alone o'er steeps and foaming falls to lean;
This is not solitude – 'tis but to hold
Converse with Nature's charms, and view her stores
   unrolled.

But midst the crowd, the hum, the shock of men,
To hear, to see, to feel, and to possess,
And roam along, the World's tired denizen,
With none who bless us, none whom we can bless;
Minions of Splendour shrinking from distress!
None that, with kindred consciousness endued,
If we were not, would seem to smile the less
Of all that flattered – followed – sought, and sued;
This is to be alone – This, This is Solitude!

And Thou Art Dead, as Young and Fair

'*Heu, quanto minus est cum reliquis versari quam tui meminisse!*'

I

And thou art dead, as young and fair
    As aught of mortal birth;
And form so soft, and charms so rare,
    Too soon return'd to Earth!
Though Earth received them in her bed,
And o'er the spot the crowd may tread
    In carelessness or mirth,
There is an eye which could not brook
A moment on that grave to look.

II

I will not ask where thou liest low,
    Nor gaze upon the spot;
There flowers or weeds at will may grow,
    So I behold them not:
It is enough for me to prove
That what I loved, and long must love,
    Like common earth can rot;
To me there needs no stone to tell,
'Tis Nothing that I loved so well.

III

Yet did I love thee to the last
    As fervently as thou,
Who didst not change through all the past,
    And canst not alter now.
The love where Death has set his seal,

Nor age can chill, nor rival steal,
        Nor falsehood disavow:
And, what were worse, thou canst not see
Or wrong, or change, or fault in me.

IV

The better days of life were ours;
        The worst can be but mine:
The sun that cheers, the storm that lowers,
        Shall never more be thine.
The silence of that dreamless sleep
I envy now too much to weep;
        Nor need I to repine,
That all those charms have pass'd away,
I might have watch'd through long decay.

V

The flower in ripen'd bloom unmatch'd
        Must fall the earliest prey;
Though by no hand untimely snatch'd,
        The leaves must drop away:
And yet it were a greater grief
To watch it withering, leaf by leaf,
        Than see it pluck'd today;
Since earthy eye but ill can bear
To trace the change to foul from fair.

VI

I know not if I could have borne
        To see thy beauties fade;
The night that follow'd such a morn
        Had worn a deeper shade:

The day without a cloud hath pass'd,
And thou wert lovely to the last;
        Extinguish'd, not decay'd;
As stars that shoot along the sky
Shine brightest as they fall from high.

VII

As once I wept, if I could weep,
        My tears might well be shed,
To think I was not near to keep
        One vigil o'er thy bed;
To gaze, how fondly! on thy face,
To fold thee in a faint embrace,
        Uphold thy drooping head;
And show that love, however vain,
Nor thou nor I can feel again.

VIII

Yet how much less it were to gain,
        Though thou hast left me free,
The loveliest things that still remain,
        Than thus remember thee!
The all of thine that cannot die
Through dark and dread Eternity
        Returns again to me,
And more thy buried love endears
Than aught, except its living years.

To Inez (from *Childe Harold's Pilgrimage*, Canto I)

Nay, smile not at my sullen brow,
　　Alas! I cannot smile again:
Yet Heaven avert that ever thou
　　Shouldst weep, and haply weep in vain.

And dost thou ask what secret woe
　　I bear, corroding Joy and Youth?
And wilt thou vainly seek to know
　　A pang ev'n thou must fail to soothe?

It is not love, it is not hate,
　　Nor low Ambition's honours lost,
That bids me loathe my present state,
　　And fly from all I prized the most:

It is that weariness which springs
　　From all I meet, or hear, or see:
To me no pleasure Beauty brings;
　　Thine eyes have scarce a charm for me.

It is that settled, ceaseless gloom
　　The fabled Hebrew Wanderer bore,
That will not look beyond the tomb,
　　But cannot hope for rest before.

What Exile from himself can flee?
　　To zones, though more and more remote,
Still, still pursues, where'er I be,
　　The blight of Life – the Demon Thought.

Yet others rapt in pleasure seem,
      And taste of all that I forsake;
Oh! may they still of transport dream,
      And ne'er – at least like me – awake!

Through many a clime 'tis mine to go,
      With many a retrospection curst;
And all my solace is to know,
      Whate'er betides, I've known the worst.

What is that worst? Nay, do not ask –
      In pity from the search forbear:
Smile on – nor venture to unmask
      Man's heart, and view the Hell that's there.

Night (from *Childe Harold's Pilgrimage*, Canto II)

'Tis night, when Meditation bids us feel
We once have loved, though Love is at an end:
The Heart, lone mourner of its baffled zeal,
Though friendless now, will dream it had a friend.
Who with the weight of years would wish to bend,
When Youth itself survives young Love and Joy?
Alas! when mingling souls forget to blend,
Death hath but little left him to destroy!
Ah! happy years! once more who would not be a boy?

Thus bending o'er the vessel's laving side,
To gaze on Dian's wave-reflected sphere,
The soul forgets her schemes of Hope and Pride,
And flies unconscious o'er each backward year.
None are so desolate but something dear,
Dearer than self, possesses or possessed
A thought, and claims the homage of a tear;
A flashing pang! of which the weary breast
Would still, albeit in vain, the heavy heart divest.

An Ode to the Framers of the Frame Bill

Oh well done Lord E——n! and better Lord R——r!
    Britannia must prosper with councils like yours;
HAWKESBURY, HARROWBY, help you to guide her,
    Whose remedy only must kill ere it cures:
Those villains; the Weavers, are all grown refractory,
    Asking some succour for Charity's sake –
So hang them in clusters round each Manufactory,
    That will at once put an end to mistake.

The rascals, perhaps, may betake them to robbing,
    The dogs to be sure have got nothing to eat –
So if we can hang them for breaking a bobbin,
    'Twill save all the Government's money and meat:
Men are more easily made than machinery –
    Stockings fetch better prices than lives –
Gibbets on Sherwood will heighten the scenery,
    Showing how Commerce, how Liberty thrives!

Justice is now in pursuit of the wretches,
    Grenadiers, Volunteers, Bow-street Police,
Twenty-two Regiments, a score of Jack Ketches,
    Three of the Quorum and two of the Peace;
Some Lords, to be sure, would have summoned the
    Judges,
    To take their opinion, but that they ne'er shall,
For LIVERPOOL such a concession begrudges,
    So now they're condemned by no Judges at all.

Some folks for certain have thought it was shocking,
    When Famine appeals, and when Poverty groans,

That life should be valued at less than a stocking,

    And breaking of frames lead to breaking of bones.

If it should prove so, I trust, by this token,

    (And who will refuse to partake in the hope?)

That the frames of the fools may be first to be *broken*,

    Who, when asked for a *remedy*, sent down a *rope*.

Lines to a Lady Weeping

Weep, daughter of a royal line,
 A Sire's disgrace, a realm's decay;
Ah! happy if each tear of thine
 Could wash a father's fault away!

Weep – for thy tears are Virtue's tears –
 Auspicious to these suffering isles;
And be each drop in future years
 Repaid thee by thy people's smiles!

A Picture of Death (from *The Giaour*)

He who hath bent him o'er the dead
Ere the first day of Death is fled,
The first dark day of Nothingness,
The last of Danger and Distress,
(Before Decay's effacing fingers
Have swept the lines where Beauty lingers)
And marked the mild angelic air,
The rapture of Repose that's there,
The fixed yet tender traits that streak
The languor of the placid cheek,
And — but for that sad shrouded eye,
That fires not, wins not, weeps not, now,
And but for that chill, changeless brow,
Where cold Obstruction's apathy
Apalls the gazing mourner's heart,
As if to him it could impart
The doom he dreads, yet dwells upon;
Yes, but for these and these alone,
Some moments, aye, one treacherous hour,
He still might doubt the Tyrant's power;
So fair, so calm, so softly sealed,
The first, last look by Death revealed!
Such is the aspect of this shore;
'Tis Greece, but living Greece no more!
So coldly sweet, so deadly fair,
We start, for Soul is wanting there.
Hers is the loveliness in death,
That parts not quite with parting breath;
But beauty with that fearful bloom,
That hue which haunts it to the tomb,

Expression's last receding ray,
A gilded Halo hovering round decay,
The farewell beam of Feeling past away!
Spark of that flame, perchance of heavenly birth,
Which gleams, but warms no more its cherished earth!

Remember Thee! Remember Thee!

I

Remember thee! remember thee!
 Till Lethe quench life's burning stream
Remorse and Shame shall cling to thee,
 And haunt thee like a feverish dream!

II

Remember thee! Aye, doubt it not.
 Thy husband too shall think of thee:
By neither shalt thou be forgot,
 Thou *false* to him, thou *fiend* to me!

Journey and Death of Hassan (from *The Giaour*)

Stern Hassan hath a journey ta'en
With twenty vassals in his train,
Each arm'd, as best becomes a man,
With arquebuss and ataghan;
The chief before, as deck'd for war,
Bears in his belt the scimitar
Stain'd with the best of Arnaut blood,
When in the pass the rebels stood,
And few return'd to tell the tale
Of what befell in Parne's vale.
The pistols which his girdle bore
Were those that once a Pasha wore,
Which still, though gemm'd and boss'd with gold,
Even robbers tremble to behold. –
'Tis said he goes to woo a bride
More true than her who left his side;
The faithless slave that broke her bower,
And – worse than faithless – for a Giaour! –

* * * * *

The sun's last rays are on the hill,
And sparkle in the fountain rill,
Whose welcome waters, cool and clear,
Draw blessings from the mountaineer;
Here may the loitering merchant Greek
Find that repose 'twere vain to seek
In cities lodg'd too near his lord,
And trembling for his secret hoard –
Here may he rest where none can see,

In crowds a slave, in desarts free;
And with forbidden wine may stain
The bowl a Moslem must not drain. –

* * * * *

    The foremost Tartar's in the gap
Conspicuous by his yellow cap,
The rest in lengthening line the while
Wind slowly through the long defile;
Above, the mountain rears a peak,
Where vultures whet the thirsty beak,
And theirs may be a feast to-night,
Shall tempt them down ere morrow's light.
Beneath, a river's wintry stream
Has shrunk before the summer beam,
And left a channel bleak and bare,
Save shrubs that spring to perish there.
Each side the midway path there lay
Small broken crags of granite grey,
By time or mountain lightning riven,
From summits clad in mists of heaven;
For where is he that hath beheld
The peak of Liakura unveil'd?

* * * * *

    They reach the grove of pine at last,
'Bismillah! now the peril's past;
For yonder view the opening plain,
And there we'll prick our steeds amain':
The Chiaus spake, and as he said,

A bullet whistled o'er his head;
The foremost Tartar bites the ground!
    Scarce had they time to check the rein,
Swift from their steeds the riders bound,
    But three shall never mount again;
Unseen the foes that gave the wound,
    The dying ask revenge in vain.
With steel unsheath'd, and carbine bent,
Some o'er their courser's harness leant,
    Half shelter'd by the steed,
Some fly behind the nearest rock,
And there await the coming shock,
    Nor tamely stand to bleed
Beneath the shaft of foes unseen,
Who dare not quit their craggy screen.
Stern Hassan only from his horse
Disdains to light, and keeps his course,
Till fiery flashes in the van
Proclaim too sure the robber-clan
Have well secur'd the only way
Could now avail the promis'd prey;
Then curl'd his very beard with ire,
And glared his eye with fiercer fire.
'Though far and near the bullets hiss,
I've 'scaped a bloodier hour than this.'
And now the foe their covert quit,
And call his vassals to submit;
But Hassan's frown and furious word
Are dreaded more than hostile sword,
Nor of his little band a man
Resign'd carbine or ataghan –
Nor raised the craven cry, Amaun!

In fuller sight, more near and near,
The lately ambush'd foes appear,
And, issuing from the grove, advance
Some who on battle-charger prance. —
Who leads them on with foreign brand,
Far flashing in his red right hand?
''Tis he! — 'tis he! — I know him now,
I know him by his pallid brow;
I know him by the evil eye
That aids his envious treachery;
I know him by his jet-black barb;
Though now array'd in Arnaut garb,
Apostate from his own vile faith,
It shall not save him from the death;
'Tis he! well met in any hour,
Lost Leila's love — accursed Giaour!'

    As rolls the river into ocean,
In sable torrent wildly streaming;
    As the sea-tide's opposing motion
In azure column proudly gleaming,
Beats back the current many a rood,
In curling foam and mingling flood;
While eddying whirl, and breaking wave,
Roused by the blast of winter rave;
Through sparkling spray in thundering clash,
The lightnings of the waters flash
In awful whiteness o'er the shore,
That shines and shakes beneath the roar;
Thus — as the stream and ocean greet,
With waves that madden as they meet —
Thus join the bands whom mutual wrong,

And fate and fury drive along.
The bickering sabres' shivering jar;
   And pealing wide — or ringing near,
   Its echoes on the throbbing ear,
The deathshot hissing from afar —
The shock — the shout — the groan of war —
   Reverberate along that vale,
   More suited to the shepherd's tale:
Though few the numbers — theirs the strife,
That neither spares nor speaks for life!
Ah! fondly youthful hearts can press,
To seize and share the dear caress;
But Love itself could never pant
For all that Beauty sighs to grant,
With half the fervour Hate bestows
Upon the last embrace of foes,
When grappling in the fight they fold
Those arms that ne'er shall lose their hold;
Friends meet to part — Love laughs at faith; —
True foes, once met, are joined till death!

* * * * *

   With sabre shiver'd to the hilt,
Yet dripping with the blood he spilt;
Yet strain'd within the sever'd hand
Which quivers round that faithless brand;
His turban far behind him roll'd,
And cleft in twain its firmest fold;
His flowing robe by falchion torn,
And crimson as those clouds of morn
That, streak'd with dusky red, portend

The day shall have a stormy end;
A stain on every bush that bore
A fragment of his palampore;
His breast with wounds unnumber'd riven,
His back to earth, his face to Heaven,
Fall'n Hassan lies – his unclos'd eye
Yet lowering on his enemy,
As if the hour that seal'd his fate
Surviving left his quenchless hate;
And o'er him bends that foe with brow
As dark as his that bled below. –

Death of Selim (from *The Bride of Abydos*, Canto II)

Zuleika, mute and motionless,
Stood like that Statue of Distress,
When, her last hope for ever gone,
The Mother harden'd into stone;
All in the maid that eye could see
Was but a younger Niobé.
But ere her lip, or even her eye,
Essayed to speak, or look reply,
Beneath the garden's wicket porch
Far flashed on high a blazing torch!
Another – and another – and another –
'Oh! fly – no more – yet now my more than brother!'
Far, wide, through every thicket spread,
The fearful lights are gleaming red;
Nor these alone – for each right hand
Is ready with a sheathless brand.
They part – pursue – return, and wheel
With searching flambeau, shining steel;
And last of all, his sabre waving,
Stern Giaffir in his fury raving:
And now almost they touch the cave –
Oh! must that grot be Selim's grave?

Dauntless he stood – ''Tis come – soon past –
One kiss, Zuleika – 'tis my last:
        But yet my band not far from shore
May hear this signal, see the flash;
Yet now too few – the attempt were rash:
        No matter – yet one effort more.'
Forth to the cavern mouth he stept;

His pistol's echo rang on high,
Zuleika started not, nor wept,
        Despair benumbed her breast and eye! –
'They hear me not, or if they ply
Their oars, 'tis but to see me die;
That sound hath drawn my foes more nigh.
Then forth my father's scimitar,
Thou ne'er hast seen less equal war!
Farewell, Zuleika! – Sweet! retire:
        Yet stay within – here linger safe,
        At thee his rage will only chafe.
Stir not – lest even to thee perchance
Some erring blade or ball should glance.
Fear'st thou for him? – may I expire
If in this strife I seek thy sire!
No – though by him that poison poured:
No – though again he call me coward!
But tamely shall I meet their steel?
No – as each crest save his may feel!'

One bound he made, and gained the sand:
        Already at his feet hath sunk
The foremost of the prying band,
        A gasping head, a quivering trunk:
Another falls – but round him close
A swarming circle of his foes;
From right to left his path he cleft,
        And almost met the meeting wave:
        His boat appears – not five oars' length –
His comrades strain with desperate strength –
        Oh! are they yet in time to save?
        His feet the foremost breakers lave;

His band are plunging in the bay,
Their sabres glitter through the spray;
Wet – wild – unwearied to the strand
They struggle – now they touch the land!
They come – 'tis but to add to slaughter –
His heart's best blood is on the water.

Escaped from shot, unharmed by steel,
Or scarcely grazed its force to feel,
Had Selim won, betrayed, beset,
To where the strand and billows met;
There as his last step left the land,
And the last death-blow dealt his hand –
Ah! wherefore did he turn to look
  For her his eye but sought in vain?
That pause, that fatal gaze he took,
  Hath doomed his death, or fixed his chain.
Sad proof, in peril and in pain,
How late will Lover's hope remain!
His back was to the dashing spray;
Behind, but close, his comrades lay,
When at the instant, hiss'd the ball –
'So may the foes of Giaffir fall!'
Whose voice is heard? whose carbine rang?
Whose bullet through the night-air sang,
Too nearly, deadly aimed to err?
'Tis thine – Abdallah's Murderer!
The father slowly rued thy hate,
The son hath found a quicker fate:
Fast from his breast the blood is bubbling,
The whiteness of the sea-foam troubling –

If aught his lips essayed to groan,
The rushing billows chocked the tone!

Morn slowly rolls the clouds away;
    Few trophies of the fight are there:
The shouts that shook the midnight-bay
Are silent; but some signs of fray
    That strand of strife may bear,
And fragments of each shivered brand;
Steps stamped; and dashed into the sand
The print of many a struggling hand
    May there be marked; nor far remote
    A broken torch, an oarless boat;
And, tangled on the weeds that heap
The beach where shelving to the deep,
    There lies a white capote!
'Tis rent in twain – one dark-red stain
The wave yet ripples o'er in vain:
    But where is he who wore?
Ye! who would o'er his relics weep,
Go, seek them where the surges sweep
Their burthen round Sigæum's steep
    And cast on Lemnos' shore:
The sea-birds shriek above the prey,
O'er which their hungry beaks delay,
As shaken on his restless pillow,
His head heaves with the heaving billow;
That hand, whose motion is not life,
Yet feebly seems to menace strife,
Flung by the tossing tide on high,
    Then levelled with the wave –

What recks it, though that corse shall lie
    Within a living grave?
The bird that tears that prostrate form
Hath only robbed the meaner worm;
The only heart, the only eye
Had bled or wept to see him die,
Had seen those scattered limbs composed,
    And mourned above his turban-stone,
That heart hath burst – that eye was closed –
    Yea – closed before his own!

Corsair Life (from *The Corsair*, Canto I)

O'er the glad waters of the dark blue sea,
Our thoughts as boundless, and our souls as free,
Far as the breeze can bear, the billows foam,
Survey our empire, and behold our home!
These are our realms, no limits to their sway –
Our flag the sceptre all who meet obey.
Ours the wild life in tumult still to range
From toil to rest, and joy in every change.
Oh, who can tell? not thou, luxurious slave!
Whose soul would sicken o'er the heaving wave;
Not thou, vain lord of wantonness and ease!
Whom slumber soothes not–pleasure cannot please –
Oh, who can tell, save he whose heart hath tried,
And danced in triumph o'er the waters wide,
The exulting sense – the pulse's maddening play,
That thrills the wanderer of that trackless way?
That for itself can woo the approaching fight,
And turn what some deem danger to delight;
That seeks what cravens shun with more than zeal,
And where the feebler faint can only feel –
Feel – to the rising bosom's inmost core,
Its hope awaken and its spirit soar?
No dread of death – if with us die our foes –
Save that it seems even duller than repose:
Come when it will – we snatch the life of life –
When lost – what recks it – by disease or strife?
Let him who crawls enamour'd of decay
Cling to his couch, and sicken years away;
Heave his thick breath, and shake his palsied head;
Ours – the fresh turf, and not the feverish bed.

While gasp by gasp he falters forth his soul,
Ours with one pang – one bound – escapes control.
His corse may boast its urn and narrow cave,
And they who loathed his life may gild his grave:
Ours are the tears, though few, sincerely shed,
When Ocean shrouds and sepulchres our dead.
For us, even banquets fond regret supply
In the red cup that crowns our memory;
And the brief epitaph in danger's day,
When those who win at length divide the prey,
And cry, Remembrance saddening o'er each brow,
How had the brave who fell exulted now!

Ode to Napoleon Buonaparte

I

'Tis done – but yesterday a King!
    And armed with Kings to strive –
And now thou art a nameless thing:
    So abject – yet alive!
Is this the man of thousand thrones,
Who strewed our earth with hostile bones,
    And can he thus survive?
Since he, miscall'd the Morning Star,
Nor man nor fiend hath fall'n so far.

II

Ill-minded man! why scourge thy kind
    Who bowed so low the knee?
By gazing on thyself grown blind,
    Thou taught'st the rest to see.
With might unquestioned, – power to save, –
Thine only gift hath been the grave
    To those that worshipp'd thee;
Nor till thy fall could mortals guess
Ambition's less than littleness!

III

Thanks for that lesson – it will teach
    To after-warriors more
Than high Philosophy can preach,
    And vainly preach'd before.
That spell upon the minds of men
Breaks never to unite again,
    That led them to adore

Those Pagod things of sabre-sway,
With fronts of brass, and feet of clay.

IV

The triumph, and the vanity,
        The rapture of the strife –
The earthquake voice of Victory,
        To thee the breath of life;
The sword, the sceptre, and that sway
Which man seem'd made but to obey,
        Wherewith renown was rife –
All quell'd! – Dark Spirit! what must be
The madness of thy memory!

V

The Desolator desolate!
        The Victor overthrown!
The Arbiter of others' fate
        A Suppliant for his own!
Is it some yet imperial hope
That with such change can calmly cope?
        Or dread of death alone?
To die a prince – or live a slave –
Thy choice is most ignobly brave!

VI

He who of old would rend the oak,
        Dreamed not of the rebound;
Chained by the trunk he vainly broke –
        Alone – how looked he round?
Thou, in the sternness of thy strength,
An equal deed hast done at length,

And darker fate hast found:
He fell, the forest prowlers' prey;
But thou must eat thy heart away!

VII

The Roman, when his burning heart
    Was slaked with blood of Rome,
Threw down the dagger – dared depart,
    In savage grandeur, home. –
He dared depart in utter scorn
Of men that such a yoke had borne,
    Yet left him such a doom!
His only glory was that hour
Of self-upheld abandon'd power.

VIII

The Spaniard, when the lust of sway
    Had lost its quickening spell,
Cast crowns for rosaries away,
    An empire for a cell;
A strict accountant of his beads,
A subtle disputant on creeds,
    His dotage trifled well:
Yet better had he neither known
A bigot's shrine, nor despot's throne.

IX

But thou – from thy reluctant hand
    The thunderbolt is wrung –
Too late thou leav'st the high command
    To which thy weakness clung;
All Evil Spirit as thou art,

It is enough to grieve the heart,
    To see thine own unstrung;
To think that God's fair world hath been
The footstool of a thing so mean;

                        X

And Earth hath spilt her blood for him,
    Who thus can hoard his own!
And Monarchs bowed the trembling limb,
    And thanked him for a throne!
Fair Freedom! we may hold thee dear,
When thus thy mightiest foes their fear
    In humblest guise have shown.
Oh! ne'er may tyrant leave behind
A brighter name to lure mankind!

                        XI

Thine evil deeds are writ in gore,
    Nor written thus in vain –
Thy triumphs tell of fame no more,
    Or deepen every stain:
If thou hadst died as honour dies,
Some new Napoleon might arise,
    To shame the world again –
But who would soar the solar height,
To set in such a starless night?

                        XII

Weigh'd in the balance, hero dust
    Is vile as vulgar clay;
Thy scales, Mortality! are just
    To all that pass away;

But yet methought the living great
Some higher sparks should animate,
    To dazzle and dismay;
Nor deem'd Contempt could thus make mirth
Of these, the Conquerors of the earth.

XIII

And she, proud Austria's mournful flower,
    Thy still imperial bride;
How bears her breast the torturing hour?
    Still clings she to thy side?
Must she too bend, must she too share
Thy late repentance, long despair,
    Thou throneless Homicide?
If still she loves thee, hoard that gem,
'Tis worth thy vanished diadem!

XIV

Then haste thee to thy sullen Isle,
    And gaze upon the sea;
That element may meet thy smile –
    It ne'er was ruled by thee!
Or trace with thine all idle hand
In loitering mood upon the sand
    That Earth is now as free!
That Corinth's pedagogue hath now
Transferred his by-word to thy brow.

XV

Thou Timour! in his captive's cage
    What thoughts will there be thine,
While brooding in thy prisoned rage?

But one – 'The world *was* mine!'
Unless, like he of Babylon,
All sense is with thy sceptre gone,
    Life will not long confine
That spirit poured so widely forth –
So long obeyed – so little worth!

XVI

Or, like the thief of fire from heaven,
    Wilt thou withstand the shock?
And share with him, the unforgiven,
    His vulture and his rock!
Foredoomed by God – by man accurst,
And that last act, though not thy worst,
    The very Fiend's arch mock;
He in his fall preserv'd his pride,
And, if a mortal, had as proudly died!

XVII

There was a day – there was an hour,
    While earth was Gaul's – Gaul thine –
When that immeasurable power
    Unsated to resign
Had been an act of purer fame
Than gathers round Marengo's name
    And gilded thy decline
Through the long twilight of all time,
Despite some passing clouds of crime.

XVIII

But thou forsooth must be a Ling
    And don the purple vest,

As if that foolish robe could wring
    Remembrance from thy breast.
Where is that faded garment? where
The gewgaws thou wert fond to wear,
    The star, the string, the crest?
Vain froward child of Empire! say,
Are all thy playthings snatched away?

XIX

Where may the wearied eye repose
    When gazing on the Great;
Where neither guilty glory glows,
    Nor despicable state?
Yes − One − the first − the last − the best −
The Cincinnatus of the West,
    Whom Envy dared not hate,
Bequeathed the name of Washington,
To make man blush there was but one!

Stanzas For Music (I speak not, I trace not, I breathe not thy name)

I speak not, I trace not, I breathe not thy name,
There is grief in the sound, there is guilt in the fame:
But the tear which now burns on my cheek may impart
The deep thoughts that dwell in that silence of heart.

Too brief for our passion, too long for our peace,
Were those hours – can their joy or their bitterness cease?
We repent, we abjure, we will break from our chain, –
We will part, we will fly to – unite it again!

Oh! thine be the gladness, and mine be the guilt!
Forgive me, adored one! – forsake, if thou wilt; –
But the heart which is thine shall expire undebased
And man shall not break it – whatever thou mayst.

And stern to the haughty, but humble to thee,
This soul, in its bitterest blackness, shall be:
And our days seem as swift, and our moments more
    sweet,
With thee by my side, than with worlds at our feet.

One sigh of thy sorrow, one look of thy love,
Shall turn me or fix, shall reward or reprove;
And the heartless may wonder at all I resign –
Thy lip shall reply, not to them, but to mine.

The Vision of Belshazzar

The King was on his throne,
　　The Satraps thronged the hall:
A thousand bright lamps shone
　　O'er that high festival.
A thousand cups of gold,
　　In Judah deemed divine —
Jehovah's vessels hold
　　The godless Heathen's wine!

In that same hour and hall,
　　The fingers of a hand
Came forth against the wall,
　　And wrote as if on sand:
The fingers of a man; —
　　A solitary hand
Along the letters ran,
　　And traced them like a wand.

The monarch saw, and shook,
　　And bade no more rejoice;
All bloodless waxed his look,
　　And tremulous his voice.
'Let the men of lore appear,
　　The wisest of the earth,
And expound the words of fear,
　　Which mar our royal mirth.'

Chaldea's seers are good,
　　But here they have no skill;
And the unknown letters stood

Untold and awful still.
And Babel's men of age
	Are wise and deep in lore;
But now they were not sage,
	They saw – but knew no more.

A captive in the land,
	A stranger and a youth,
He heard the King's command,
	He saw that writing's truth.
The lamps around were bright,
	The prophecy in view;
He read it on that night, –
	The morrow proved it true.

'Belshazzar's grave is made,
	His kingdom passed away,
He, in the balance weighed,
	Is light and worthless clay;
The shroud, his robe of state,
	His canopy the stone;
The Mede is at his gate!
	The Persian on his throne!'

She Walks in Beauty

I

She walks in Beauty, like the night
 Of cloudless climes and starry skies;
And all that's best of dark and bright
 Meet in her aspect and her eyes:
Thus mellowed to that tender light
 Which Heaven to gaudy day denies.

II

One shade the more, one ray the less,
 Had half impaired the nameless grace
Which waves in every raven tress,
 Or softly lightens o'er her face;
Where thoughts serenely sweet express,
 How pure, how dear their dwelling-place.

awww someones got a crush!

III

And on that cheek, and o'er that brow,
 So soft, so calm, yet eloquent,
The smiles that win, the tints that glow,
 But tell of days in goodness spent,
A mind at peace with all below,
 A heart whose love is innocent!

Greece (from *The Corsair*, Canto III)

Slow sinks, more lovely ere his race be run,
Along Morea's hills the setting Sun;
Not, as in northern climes, obscurely bright,
But one unclouded blaze of living light!
O'er the hush'd deep the yellow beam he throws,
Gilds the green wave that trembles as it glows;
On old Ægina's rock, and Idra's isle
The God of gladness sheds his parting smile;
O'er his own regions lingering, loves to shine,
Though there his altars are no more divine.
Descending fast the mountain-shadows kiss
Thy glorious gulf, unconquered Salamis!
Their azure arches through the long expanse,
More deeply purpled, meet his mellowing glance,
And tenderest tints, along their summits driven,
Mark his gay course, and own the hues of Heaven;
Till, darkly shaded from the land and deep,
Behind his Delphian rock he sinks to sleep.

On such an eve, his palest beam he cast
When – Athens! here thy Wisest looked his last.
How watched thy better sons his farewell ray,
That closed their murdered Sage's latest day!
Not yet – not yet – Sol pauses on the hill,
The precious hour of parting lingers still;
But sad his light to agonising eyes,
And dark the mountain's once delightful dyes:
Gloom o'er the lovely land he seemed to pour,
The land where Phœbus never frowned before;
But ere he sunk below Cithæron's head,

The cup of woe was quaffed – the Spirit fled;
The soul of him that scorned to fear or fly –
Who lived and died, as none can live or die!

But, lo! from high Hymettus to the plain,
The queen of night asserts her silent reign.
No murky vapour, herald of the storm,
Hides her fair face, nor girds her glowing form;
With cornice glimmering as the moon-beams play,
There the white column greets her grateful ray,
And bright around with quivering beams beset,
Her emblem sparkles o'er the Minaret:
The groves of olive scattered dark and wide
Where meek Cephisus sheds his scanty tide,
The cypress saddening by the sacred Mosque,
The gleaming turret of the gay Kiosk;
And, dun and sombre 'mid the holy calm,
Near Theseus' fane, yon solitary palm,
All tinged with varied hues arrest the eye –
And dull were his that passed them heedless by.

Again the Ægean, heard no more afar,
Lulls his chafed breast from elemental war;
Again his waves in milder tints unfold
Their long expanse of sapphire and of gold,
Mixed with the shades of many a distant isle,
That frown, where gentler Ocean seems to smile.

agreed music is my medicine

Stanzas for Music (There's not a joy the world can give like that it takes away)

I

There's not a joy the world can give like that it takes
    away,
When the glow of early thought declines in Feeling's dull
    decay;
'Tis not on Youth's smooth cheek the blush alone, which
    fades so fast,
But the tender bloom of heart is gone, ere Youth itself be
    past.

II

Then the few whose spirits float above the wreck of
    happiness
Are driven o'er the shoals of guilt or ocean of excess:
The magnet of their course is gone, or only points in vain
The shore to which their shivered sail shall never stretch
    again.

III

Then the mortal coldness of the soul like Death itself
    comes down;
It cannot feel for others' woes, it dare not dream its own;
That heavy chill has frozen o'er the fountain of our tears,
And though the eye may sparkle still, 'tis where the ice
    appears.

IV

Though wit may flash from fluent lips, and mirth distract
    the breast,
Through midnight hours that yield no more their former
    hope of rest;
'Tis but as ivy-leaves around the ruined turret wreath,
All green and wildly fresh without, but worn and grey
    beneath.

V

Oh, could I feel as I have felt, – or be what I have been,
Or weep as I could once have wept, o'er many a vanished
    scene;
As springs in deserts found seem sweet, all brackish
    though they be,
So, midst the withered waste of life, those tears would
    flow to me.

The Destruction of Sennacherib

I

The Assyrian came down like the wolf on the fold,
And his cohorts were gleaming in purple and gold;
And the sheen of their spears was like stars on the sea,
When the blue wave rolls nightly on deep Galilee.

II

Like the leaves of the forest when Summer is green,
That host with their banners at sunset were seen:
Like the leaves of the forest when Autumn hath blown,
That host on the morrow lay withered and strown.

III

For the Angel of Death spread his wings on the blast,
And breathed in the face of the foe as he passed;
And the eyes of the sleepers waxed deadly and chill,
And their hearts but once heaved, and for ever grew still!

IV

And there lay the steed with his nostril all wide,
But through it there rolled not the breath of his pride;
And the foam of his gasping lay white on the turf,
And cold as the spray of the rock-beating surf.

V

And there lay the rider distorted and pale,
With the dew on his brow, and the rust on his mail:
And the tents were all silent, the banners alone,
The lances unlifted, the trumpet unblown.

VI

And the widows of Ashur are loud in their wail,
And the idols are broke in the temple of Baal;
And the might of the Gentile, unsmote by the sword,
Hath melted like snow in the glance of the Lord!

Song of Saul Before His Last Battle

Warriors and chiefs! should the shaft or the sword
Pierce me in leading the host of the Lord,
Heed not the corse, though a king's, in your path:
Bury your steel in the bosoms of Gath!

Thou who art bearing my buckler and bow,
Should the soldiers of Saul look away from the foe,
Stretch me that moment in blood at thy feet!
Mine be the doom which they dared not to meet.

Farewell to others, but never we part,
Heir to my royalty, son of my heart!
Bright is the diadem, boundless the sway,
Or kingly the death, which awaits us today!

Why is losing your
life in battle
so honorable?
and
venerable

Oh! Snatch'd Away

I

Oh! snatched away in beauty's bloom,
On thee shall press no ponderous tomb;
 But on thy turf shall roses rear
 Their leaves, the earliest of the year;
And the wild cypress wave in tender gloom:

II

And oft by yon blue gushing stream
 Shall Sorrow lean her drooping head,
And feed deep thought with many a dream,
 And lingering pause and lightly tread;
 Fond wretch! as if her step disturbed the dead!

III

Away! we know that tears are vain,
 That Death nor heeds nor hears distress:
Will this unteach us to complain?
 Or make one mourner weep the less?
And thou – who tell'st me to forget,
Thy looks are wan, thine eyes are wet.

Napoleon's Farewell

From the French

I

Farewell to the Land, where the gloom of my Glory
Arose and o'ershadowed the earth with her name –
She abandons me now – but the page of her story,
The brightest or blackest, is filled with my fame.
I have warred with a World which vanquished me only
When the meteor of conquest allured me too far;
I have coped with the nations which dread me thus
    lonely,
The last single Captive to millions in war.

II

Farewell to thee, France! when thy diadem crowned me,
I made thee the gem and the wonder of earth, –
But thy weakness decrees I should leave as I found thee,
Decayed in thy glory, and sunk in thy worth.
Oh! for the veteran hearts that were wasted
In strife with the storm, when their battles were won –
Then the Eagle, whose gaze in that moment was blasted
Had still soared with eyes fixed on Victory's sun!

III

Farewell to thee, France! – but when Liberty rallies
Once more in thy regions, remember me then, –
The violet still grows in the depth of thy valleys;
Though withered, thy tear will unfold it again –
Yet, yet, I may baffle the hosts that surround us,
And yet may thy heart leap awake to my voice –

There are links which must break in the chain that has
   bound us,
Then turn thee and call on the Chief of thy choice!

interesting.—

From the French

I

Must thou go, my glorious Chief,
    Severed from thy faithful few?
Who can tell thy warrior's grief,
    Maddening o'er that long adieu?
Woman's love, and Friendship's zeal,
    Dear as both have been to me –
What are they to all I feel,
    With a soldier's faith for thee?

II

Idol of the soldier's soul!
    First in fight, but mightiest now;
Many could a world control;
    Thee alone no doom can bow.
By thy side for years I dared
    Death; and envied those who fell,
When their dying shout was heard,
    Blessing him they served so well.

III

Would that I were cold with those,
    Since this hour I live to see;
When the doubts of coward foes
    Scarce dare trust a man with thee,
Dreading each should set thee free!
    Oh! although in dungeons pent,
All their chains were light to me,
    Gazing on thy soul unbent.

IV

Would the sycophants of him
>   Now so deaf to duty's prayer,
Were his borrowed glories dim,
>   In his native darkness share?
Were that world this hour his own,
>   All thou calmly dost resign,
Could he purchase with that throne
>   Hearts like those which still are thine?

V

My Chief, my King, my Friend, adieu!
>   Never did I droop before;
Never to my Sovereign sue,
>   As his foes I now implore:
All I ask is to divide
>   Every peril he must brave;
Sharing by the hero's side
>   His fall – his exile – and his grave.

*love
this*

Ode (from the French)

We do not curse thee, Waterloo!
Though Freedom's blood thy plain bedew;
There 'twas shed, but is not sunk —
Rising from each gory trunk,
Like the water-spout from ocean,
With a strong and growing motion —
It soars, and mingles in the air,
With that of lost La Bédoyère —
With that of him whose honoured grave
Contains the 'bravest of the brave'.
A crimson cloud it spreads and glows,
But shall return to whence it rose;
When 'tis full 'twill burst asunder —
Never yet was heard such thunder
As then shall shake the world with wonder —
Never yet was seen such lightning
As o'er heaven shall then be bright'ning!
Like the Wormwood Star foretold
⠀⠀⠀By the sainted Seer of old,
Show'ring down a fiery flood,
Turning rivers into blood.

The Chief has fallen, but not by you,
Vanquishers of Waterloo!
When the soldier citizen
Sway'd not o'er his fellow-men —
Save in deeds that led them on
Where Glory smiled on Freedom's son —
Who, of all the despots banded,
⠀⠀⠀With that youthful chief competed?

Who could boast o'er France defeated,
Till lone Tyranny commanded?
Till, goaded by Ambition's sting,
The Hero sunk into the King?
Then he fell: – so perish all,
Who would men by man enthral!

And thou, too, of the snow-white plume!
Whose realm refused thee ev'n a tomb;
Better hadst thou still been leading
France o'er hosts of hirelings bleeding,
Than sold thyself to death and shame
For a meanly royal name;
Such as he of Naples wears,
Who thy blood-bought title bears.
Little didst thou deem, when dashing
    On thy war-horse through the ranks,
    Like a stream which burst its banks,
While helmets cleft, and sables clashing,
Shone and shivered fast around thee –
Of the fate at last which found thee:
Was that haughty plume laid low
By a slave's dishonest blow?
Once – as the Moon sways o'er the tide,
It rolled in air, the warrior's guide;
Through the smoke-created night
Of the black and sulphurous fight,
The soldier raised his seeking eye
To catch that crest's ascendency, –
And, as it onward rolling rose,
So moved his heart upon our foes.
There, where death's brief pang was quickest,

And the battle's wreck lay thickest,
Strew'd beneath the advancing banner
    Of the eagle's burning crest —
(There with thunder-clouds to fan her,
      Who could then her wing arrest —
      Victory beaming from her breast?)
While the broken line enlarging
    Fell, or fled along the plain;
There be sure was Murat charging!
    There he ne'er shall charge again!

O'er glories gone the invaders march,
Weeps Triumph o'er each levell'd arch —
But let Freedom rejoice,
With her heart in her voice;
But, her hand on the sword,
Doubly shall she be adored;
France hath twice too well been taught
The 'moral lesson' dearly bought —
Her safety sits not on a throne,
With Capet or Napoleon!
But in equal rights and laws,
Hearts and hands in one great cause —
Freedom, such as God hath given
Unto all beneath his heaven,
With their breath, and from their birth,
Though guilt would sweep it from the earth —
With a fierce and lavish hand
Scattering nations' wealth like sand;
Pouring nations' blood like water,
In imperial seas of slaughter!

But the heart and the mind,
And the voice of mankind,
Shall arise in communion —
And who shall resist that proud union?
The time is past when swords subdued —
Man may die — the soul's renew'd:
Even in this low world of care
Freedom ne'er shall want an heir;
Millions breathe but to inherit
Her for ever bounding spirit —
When once more her hosts assemble,
Tyrants shall believe and tremble —
Smile they at this idle threat?
Crimson tears will follow yet.

The Prisoner of Chillon

My hair is grey, but not with years,
Nor grew it white
    In a single night,
As men's have grown from sudden fears:
My limbs are bow'd, though not with toil,
    But rusted with a vile repose,
For they have been a dungeon's spoil,
    And mine has been the fate of those
To whom the goodly earth and air
Are banned, and barred – forbidden fare;
But this was for my father's faith
I suffer'd chains and courted death;
That father perished at the stake
For tenets he would not forsake;
And for the same his lineal race
In darkness found a dwelling place;
We were seven – who now are one,
    Six in youth, and one in age,
Finished as they had begun,
    Proud of Persecution's rage;
One in fire, and two in field,
Their belief with blood have sealed,
Dying as their father died,
For the God their foes denied; –
Three were in a dungeon cast,
Of whom this wreck is left the last.

There are seven pillars of Gothic mould,
In Chillon's dungeons deep and old,
There are seven columns, massy and grey,

Dim with a dull imprisoned ray,
A sunbeam which hath lost its way,
And through the crevice and the cleft
Of the thick wall is fallen and left;
Creeping o'er the floor so damp,
Like a marsh's meteor lamp:
And in each pillar there is a ring,
　　　And in each ring there is a chain;
That iron is a cankering thing,
　　　For in these limbs its teeth remain,
With marks that will not wear away,
Till I have done with this new day,
Which now is painful to these eyes,
Which have not seen the sun so rise
For years – I cannot count them o'er,
I lost their long and heavy score
When my last brother droop'd and died,
And I lay living by his side.

They chained us each to a column stone,
And we were three – yet, each alone;
We could not move a single pace,
We could not see each other's face,
But with that pale and livid light
That made us strangers in our sight:
And thus together – yet apart,
Fettered in hand, but join'd in heart,
'Twas still some solace in the dearth
Of the pure elements of earth,
To hearken to each other's speech,
And each turn comforter to each
With some new hope, or legend old,

Or song heroically bold;
But even these at length grew cold.
Our voices took a dreary tone,
An echo of the dungeon stone,
    A grating sound, not full and free,
    As they of yore were wont to be:
    It might be fancy – but to me
They never sounded like our own.

I was the eldest of the three
    And to uphold and cheer the rest
    I ought to do – and did my best –
And each did well in his degree.
    The youngest, whom my father loved,
Because our mother's brow was given
To him, with eyes as blue as heaven –
    For him my soul was sorely moved:
And truly might it be distressed
To see such bird in such a nest;
For he was beautiful as day –
    (When day was beautiful to me
    As to young eagles, being free) –
    A polar day, which will not see
A sunset till its summer's gone,
    Its sleepless summer of long light,
The snow-clad offspring of the sun:
    And thus he was as pure and bright,
And in his natural spirit gay,
With tears for nought but others' ills,
And then they flowed like mountain rills,
Unless he could assuage the woe
Which he abhorred to view below.

The other was as pure of mind,
But formed to combat with his kind;
Strong in his frame, and of a mood
Which 'gainst the world in war had stood,
And perish'd in the foremost rank
    With joy: – but not in chains to pine:
His spirit wither'd with their clank,
    I saw it silently decline –
    And so perchance in sooth did mine:
But yet I forced it on to cheer
Those relics of a home so dear.
He was a hunter of the hills,
    Had followed there the deer and wolf;
    To him this dungeon was a gulf,
And fetter'd feet the worst of ills.

    Lake Leman lies by Chillon's walls:
A thousand feet in depth below
Its massy waters meet and flow;
Thus much the fathom-line was sent
From Chillon's snow-white battlement,
    Which round about the wave inthralls:
A double dungeon wall and wave
Have made – and like a living grave.
Below the surface of the lake
The dark vault lies wherein we lay:
We heard it ripple night and day;
    Sounding o'er our heads it knocked;
And I have felt the winter's spray
Wash through the bars when winds were high
And wanton in the happy sky;
    And then the very rock hath rocked,

And I have felt it shake, unshocked,
Because I could have smiled to see
The death that would have set me free.

I said my nearer brother pined,
I said his mighty heart declined,
He loathed and put away his food;
It was not that 'twas coarse and rude,
For we were used to hunter's fare,
And for the like had little care:
The milk drawn from the mountain goat
Was changed for water from the moat,
Our bread was such as captives' tears
Have moistened many a thousand years,
Since man first pent his fellow men
Like brutes within an iron den;
But what were these to us or him?
These wasted not his heart or limb;
My brother's soul was of that mould
Which in a palace had grown cold,
Had his free breathing been denied
The range of the steep mountain's side;
But why delay the truth? – he died.
I saw, and could not hold his head,
Nor reach his dying hand – nor dead, –
Though hard I strove, but strove in vain,
To rend and gnash my bonds in twain.
He died – and they unlocked his chain,
And scoop'd for him a shallow grave
Even from the cold earth of our cave.
I begged them, as a boon, to lay
His corse in dust whereon the day

Might shine – it was a foolish thought,
But then within my brain it wrought,
That even in death his freeborn breast
In such a dungeon could not rest.
I might have spared my idle prayer –
They coldly laughed – and laid him there:
The flat and turfless earth above
The being we so much did love;
His empty chain above it leant,
Such Murder's fitting monument!

But he, the favourite and the flower,
Most cherished since his natal hour,
His mother's image in fair face,
The infant love of all his race,
His martyr'd father's dearest thought,
My latest care, for whom I sought
To hoard my life, that his might be
Less wretched now, and one day free;
He, too, who yet had held untired
A spirit natural or inspired –
He, too, was struck, and day by day
Was wither'd on the stalk away.
Oh, God! it is a fearful thing
To see the human soul take wing
In any shape, in any mood:
I've seen it rushing forth in blood,
I've seen it on the breaking ocean
Strive with a swoln convulsive motion,
I've seen the sick and ghastly bed
Of Sin delirious with its dread:
But these were horrors – this was woe

Unmixded with such – but sure and slow:
He faded, and so calm and meek,
So softly worn, so sweetly weak,
So tearless, yet so tender – kind,
And grieved for those he left behind;
With all the while a cheek whose bloom
Was as a mockery of the tomb,
Whose tints as gently sunk away
As a departing rainbow's ray;
An eye of most transparent light,
That almost made the dungeon bright;
And not a word of murmur – not
A groan o'er his untimely lot, –
A little talk of better days,
A little hope my own to raise,
For I was sunk in silence – lost
In this last loss, of all the most;
And then the sighs he would suppress
Of fainting Nature's feebleness,
More slowly drawn, grew less and less:
I listen'd, but I could not hear;
I call'd, for I was wild with fear;
I knew 'twas hopeless, but my dread
Would not be thus admonished;
I call'd, and thought I heard a sound –
I burst my chain with one strong bound,
And rushed to him: – I found him not,
I only stirred in this black spot,
I only lived, I only drew
The accursed breath of dungeon-dew;
The last, the sole, the dearest link
Between me and the eternal brink,

Which bound me to my failing race
Was broken in this fatal place.
One on the earth, and one beneath –
My brothers – both had ceased to breathe:
I took that hand which lay so still,
Alas! my own was full as chill;
I had not strength to stir, or strive,
But felt that I was still alive –
A frantic feeling, when we know
That what we love shall ne'er be so.
      I know not why
      I could not die,
I had no earthly hope – but faith,
And that forbade a selfish death.

What next befell me then and there
      I know not well – I never knew –
First came the loss of light, and air,
      And then of darkness too:
I had no thought, no feeling – none –
Among the stones I stood a stone,
And was, scarce conscious what I wist,
As shrubless crags within the mist;
For all was blank, and bleak, and grey;
It was not night – it was not day;
It was not even the dungeon-light,
So hateful to my heavy sight,
But vacancy absorbing space,
And fixedness – without a place;
There were no stars – no earth – no time –
No check – no change – no good – no crime –
But silence, and a stirless breath

Which neither was of life nor death;
A sea of stagnant idleness,
Blind, boundless, mute, and motionless!

A light broke in upon my brain, –
    It was the carol of a bird;
It ceased, and then it came again,
    The sweetest song ear ever heard,
And mine was thankful till my eyes
Ran over with the glad surprise,
And they that moment could not see
I was the mate of misery;
But then by dull degrees came back
My senses to their wonted track;
I saw the dungeon walls and floor
Close slowly round me as before,
I saw the glimmer of the sun
Creeping as it before had done,
But through the crevice where it came
That bird was perched, as fond and tame,
    And tamer than upon the tree;
A lovely bird, with azure wings,
And song that said a thousand things,
    And seemed to say them all for me!
I never saw its like before,
I ne'er shall see its likeness more:
It seem'd like me to want a mate,
But was not half so desolate,
And it was come to love me when
None lived to love me so again,
And cheering from my dungeon's brink,
Had brought me back to feel and think.

I know not if it late were free,
        Or broke its cage to perch on mine,
But knowing well captivity,
        Sweet bird! I could not wish for thine!
Or if it were, in winged guise,
A visitant from Paradise;
For – Heaven forgive that thought! the while
Which made me both to weep and smile –
I sometimes deemed that it might be
My brother's soul come down to me;
But then at last away it flew,
And then 'twas mortal well I knew,
For he would never thus have flown –
And left me twice so doubly lone, –
Lone – as the corse within its shroud,
Lone – as a solitary cloud,
        A single cloud on a sunny day,
While all the rest of heaven is clear,
A frown upon the atmosphere,
That hath no business to appear
        When skies are blue, and earth is gay.

A kind of change came in my fate,
My keepers grew compassionate;
I know not what had made them so,
They were inured to sights of woe,
But so it was: – my broken chain
With links unfasten'd did remain,
And it was liberty to stride
Along my cell from side to side,
And up and down, and then athwart,
And tread it over every part;

And round the pillars one by one,
Returning where my walk begun,
Avoiding only, as I trod,
My brothers' graves without a sod;
For if I thought with heedless tread
My step profaned their lowly bed,
My breath came gaspingly and thick,
And my crush'd heart felt blind and sick.

I made a footing in the wall,
    It was not therefrom to escape,
For I had buried one and all,
    Who loved me in a human shape;
And the whole earth would henceforth be
A wider prison unto me:
No child – no sire – no kin had I,
No partner in my misery;
I thought of this, and I was glad,
For thought of them had made me mad;
But I was curious to ascend
To my barred windows, and to bend
Once more, upon the mountains high,
The quiet of a loving eye.

I saw them – and they were the same,
They were not changed like me in frame;
I saw their thousand years of snow
On high – their wide long lake below,
And the blue Rhone in fullest flow;
I heard the torrents leap and gush
O'er channelled rock and broken bush;
I saw the white-walled distant town,

And whiter sails go skimming down;
And then there was a little isle,
Which in my very face did smile,
    The only one in view;
A small green isle, it seemed no more,
Scarce broader than my dungeon floor,
But in it there were three tall trees,
And o'er it blew the mountain breeze,
And by it there were waters flowing,
And on it there were young flowers growing,
    Of gentle breath and hue.
The fish swam by the castle wall,
And they seem'd joyous each and all;
The eagle rode the rising blast,
Methought he never flew so fast
As then to me he seem'd to fly;
And then new tears came in my eye,
And I felt troubled – and would fain
I had not left my recent chain;
And when I did descend again,
The darkness of my dim abode
Fell on me as a heavy load;
It was as is a new-dug grave,
Closing o'er one we sought to save, –
And yet my glance, too much opprest,
Had almost need of such a rest.

It might be months, or years, or days –
    I kept no count, I took no note –
I had no hope my eyes to raise,
    And clear them of their dreary mote;
At last men came to set me free;

I asked not why, and recked not where;
It was at length the same to me,
Fettered or fetterless to be,
I learned to love despair.
And thus when they appear'd at last,
And all my bonds aside were cast,
These heavy walls to me had grown
A hermitage – and all my own!
And half I felt as they were come
To tear me from a second home:
With spiders I had friendship made,
And watched them in their sullen trade,
Had seen the mice by moonlight play,
And why should I feel less than they?
We were all inmates of one place,
And I, the monarch of each race,
Had power to kill – yet, strange to tell!
In quiet we had learned to dwell;
My very chains and I grew friends,
So much a long communion tends
To make us what we are: – even I
Regain'd my freedom with a sigh.

Fare Thee Well

'Alas! they had been friends in youth;
But whispering tongues can poison truth:
And Constancy lives in realms above;
And Life is thorny; and youth is vain:
And to be wroth with one we love,
Doth work like madness in the brain;

* * * * *

But never either found another
To free the hollow heart from paining –
They stood aloof, the scars remaining,
Like cliffs which had been rent asunder;
A dreary sea now flows between,
But neither heat, nor frost, nor thunder,
Shall wholly do away, I ween,
The marks of that which once hath been.'
    COLERIDGE'S *Christabel*.

Fare thee well! and if for ever,
    Still for ever, fare *thee well*:
Even though unforgiving, never
    'Gainst thee shall my heart rebel.
Would that breast were bared before thee
    Where thy head so oft hath lain,
While that placid sleep came o'er thee
    Which thou ne'er canst know again:
Would that breast, by thee glanced over,
    Every inmost thought could show!

Then thou would'st at last discover
    'Twas not well to spurn it so.
Though the world for this commend thee –
    Though it smile upon the blow,
Even its praises must offend thee,
    Founded on another's woe:
Though my many faults defaced me,
    Could no other arm be found,
Than the one which once embraced me,
    To inflict a cureless wound?
Yet, oh yet, thyself deceive not –
    Love may sink by slow decay,
But by sudden wrench, believe not
    Hearts can thus be torn away:
Still thine own its life retaineth –
    Still must mine, though bleeding, beat;
And the undying thought which paineth
    Is – that we no more may meet.
These are words of deeper sorrow
    Than the wail above the dead;
Both shall live – but every morrow
    Wake us from a widowed bed.
And when thou would'st solace gather –
    When our child's first accents flow –
Wilt thou teach her to say 'Father!'
    Though his care she must forego?
When her little hands shall press thee –
    When her lip to thine is pressed –
Think of him whose prayer shall bless thee –
    Think of him thy love *had* blessed!
Should her lineaments resemble
    Those thou never more may'st see,

Then thy heart will softly tremble
      With a pulse yet true to me.
All my faults perchance thou knowest –
      All my madness – none can know;
All my hopes – where'er thou goest –
      Wither – yet with thee they go.
Every feeling hath been shaken;
      Pride – which not a world could bow –
Bows to thee – by thee forsaken,
      Even my soul forsakes me now.
But 'tis done – all words are idle –
      Words from me are vainer still;
But the thoughts we cannot bridle
      Force their way without the will.
Fare thee well! thus disunited –
      Torn from every nearer tie –
Seared in heart – and lone – and blighted –
      More than this I scarce can die.

Calm on Lake Leman (from *Childe Harold's Pilgrimage*, Canto III)

Clear, placid Leman! thy contrasted lake,
With the wild world I dwelt in, is a thing
Which warns me, with its stillness, to forsake
Earth's troubled waters for a purer spring.
This quiet sail is as a noiseless wing
To waft me from distraction; once I loved
Torn Ocean's roar, but thy soft murmuring
Sounds sweet as if a Sister's voice reproved,
That I with stern delights should e'er have been so moved.

It is the hush of night, and all between
Thy margin and the mountains, dusk, yet clear,
Mellowed and mingling, yet distinctly seen,
Save darkened Jura, whose capt heights appear
Precipitously steep; and drawing near,
There breathes a living fragrance from the shore,
Of flowers yet fresh with childhood; on the ear
Drops the light drip of the suspended oar,
Or chirps the grasshopper one good-night carol more.

He is an evening reveller, who makes
His life an infancy, and sings his fill;
At intervals, some bird from out the brakes
Starts into voice a moment, then is still.
There seems a floating whisper on the hill,
But that is fancy — for the Starlight dews
All silently their tears of Love instil,
Weeping themselves away, till they infuse
Deep into Nature's breast the spirit of her hues.

The Dream

Our life is twofold; Sleep hath its own world,
A boundary between the things misnamed
Death and existence: Sleep hath its own world,
And a wide realm of wild reality,
And dreams in their development have breath,
And tears, and tortures, and the touch of Joy;
They leave a weight upon our waking thoughts,
They take a weight from off our waking toils,
They do divide our being; they become
A portion of ourselves as of our time,
And look like heralds of Eternity;
They pass like spirits of the past, – they speak
Like Sibyls of the future; they have power –
The tyranny of pleasure and of pain;
They make us what we were not – what they will,
And shake us with the vision that's gone by,
The dread of vanished shadows. – Are they so?
Is not the past all shadow? What are they?
Creations of the mind? – The mind can make
Substances, and people planets of its own
With beings brighter than have been, and give
A breath to forms which can outlive all flesh.
I would recall a vision which I dreamed
Perchance in sleep – for in itself a thought,
A slumbering thought, is capable of years,
And curdles a long life into one hour.

I saw two beings in the hues of youth
Standing upon a hill, a gentle hill,
Green and of a mild declivity, the last

As 'twere the cape of a long ridge of such,
Save that there was no sea to lave its base,
But a most living landscape, and the wave
Of woods and cornfields, and the abodes of men
Scattered at intervals, and wreathing smoke
Arising from such rustic roofs; — the hill
Was crowned with a peculiar diadem
Of trees, in circular array, so fixed,
Not by the sport of nature, but of man:
These two, a maiden and a youth, were there
Gazing — the one on all that was beneath
Fair as herself — but the Boy gazed on her;
And both were young, and one was beautiful:
And both were young — yet not alike in youth.
As the sweet moon on the horizon's verge,
The maid was on the eve of womanhood;
The boy had fewer summers, but his heart
Had far outgrown his years, and to his eye
There was but one beloved face on earth,
And that was shining on him; he had looked
Upon it till it could not pass away;
He had no breath, no being, but in hers;
She was his voice; he did not speak to her,
But trembled on her words; she was his sight,
For his eye followed hers, and saw with hers,
Which coloured all his objects: — he had ceased
To live within himself; she was his life,
The ocean to the river of his thoughts,
Which terminated all: upon a tone,
A touch of hers, his blood would ebb and flow,
And his cheek change tempestuously — his heart
Unknowing of its cause of agony.

But she in these fond feelings had no share:
Her sighs were not for him; to her he was
Even as a brother – but no more; 'twas much,
For brotherless she was, save in the name
Her infant friendship had bestowed on him;
Herself the solitary scion left
Of a time-honoured race. – It was a name
Which pleased him, and yet pleased him not – and why?
Time taught him a deep answer – when she loved
Another; even now she loved another,
And on the summit of that hill she stood,
Looking afar if yet her lover's steed
Kept pace with her expectancy, and flew.

A change came o'er the spirit of my dream.
There was an ancient mansion, and before
Its walls there was a steed caparisoned:
Within an antique Oratory stood
The Boy of whom I spake; – he was alone,
And pale, and pacing to and fro: anon
He sate him down, and seized a pen, and traced
Words which I could not guess of; then he leaned
His bowed head on his hands and shook, as 'twere
With a convulsion – then arose again,
And with his teeth and quivering hands did tear
What he had written, but he shed no tears.
And he did calm himself, and fix his brow
Into a kind of quiet: as he paused,
The Lady of his love re-entered there;
She was serene and smiling then, and yet
She knew she was by him beloved – she knew,
For quickly comes such knowledge, that his heart

Was darkened with her shadow, and she saw
That he was wretched, but she saw not all.
He rose, and with a cold and gentle grasp
He took her hand; a moment o'er his face
A tablet of unutterable thoughts
Was traced, and then it faded, as it came;
He dropped the hand he held, and with slow steps
Retired, but not as bidding her adieu,
For they did part with mutual smiles; he passed
From out the massy gate of that old Hall,
And mounting on his steed he went his way;
And ne'er repassed that hoary threshold more.

A change came o'er the spirit of my dream.
The boy was sprung to manhood: in the wilds
Of fiery climes he made himself a home,
And his Soul drank their sunbeams: he was girt
With strange and dusky aspects; he was not
Himself like what he had been; on the sea
And on the shore he was a wanderer;
There was a mass of many images
Crowded like waves upon me, but he was
A part of all; and in the last he lay
Reposing from the noontide sultriness,
Couched among fallen columns, in the shade
Of ruined walls that had survived the names
Of those who reared them; by his sleeping side
Stood camels grazing, and some goodly steeds
Were fastened near a fountain; and a man,
Clad in a flowing garb, did watch the while,
While many of his tribe slumbered around:
And they were canopied by the blue sky,

So cloudless, clear, and purely beautiful,
That God alone was to be seen in Heaven.

A change came o'er the spirit of my dream.
The Lady of his love was wed with One
Who did not love her better: – in her home,
A thousand leagues from his, – her native home,
She dwelt, begirt with growing Infancy,
Daughters and sons of Beauty, – but behold!
Upon her face there was the tint of grief,
The settled shadow of an inward strife,
And an unquiet drooping of the eye,
As if its lids were charged with unshed tears.
What could her grief be? – she had all she loved,
And he who had so loved her was not there
To trouble with bad hopes, or evil wish,
Or ill-repressed affliction, her pure thoughts.
What could her grief be? – she had loved him not,
Nor given him cause to deem himself beloved,
Nor could he be a part of that which preyed
Upon her mind – a spectre of the past.

A change came o'er the spirit of my dream.
The Wanderer was returned. – I saw him stand
Before an Altar – with a gentle bride;
Her face was fair, but was not that which made
The Starlight of his Boyhood; – as he stood
Even at the altar, o'er his brow there came
The selfsame aspect, and the quivering shock
That in the antique Oratory shook
His bosom in its solitude; and then –
As in that hour – a moment o'er his face

The tablet of unutterable thoughts
Was traced, – and then it faded as it came,
And he stood calm and quiet, and he spoke
The fitting vows, but heard not his own words,
And all things reeled around him; he could see
Not that which was, nor that which should have been –
But the old mansion, and the accustomed hall,
And the remembered chambers, and the place,
The day, the hour, the sunshine, and the shade,
All things pertaining to that place and hour,
And her who was his destiny, came back
And thrust themselves between him and the light:
What business had they there at such a time?

A change came o'er the spirit of my dream.
The Lady of his love; – Oh! she was changed,
As by the sickness of the soul; her mind
Had wandered from its dwelling, and her eyes,
They had not their own lustre, but the look
Which is not of the earth; she was become
The queen of a fantastic realm; her thoughts
Were combinations of disjointed things;
And forms impalpable and unperceived .
Of others' sight familiar were to hers.
And this the world calls frenzy; but the wise
Have a far deeper madness, and the glance
Of melancholy is a fearful gift;
What is it but the telescope of truth?
Which strips the distance of its fantasies,
And brings life near in utter nakedness,
Making the cold reality too real!

A change came o'er the spirit of my dream.
The Wanderer was alone as heretofore,
The beings which surrounded him were gone,
Or were at war with him; he was a mark
For blight and desolation, compassed round
With Hatred and Contention; Pain was mixed
In all which was served up to him, until,
Like to the Pontic monarch of old days,
He fed on poisons, and they had no power,
But were a kind of nutriment; he lived
Through that which had been death to many men,
And made him friends of mountains: with the stars
And the quick Spirit of the Universe
He held his dialogues; and they did teach
To him the magic of their mysteries;
To him the book of Night was opened wide,
And voices from the deep abyss revealed
A marvel and a secret — Be it so.

My dream was past; it had no further change.
It was of a strange order, that the doom
Of these two creatures should be thus traced out
Almost like a reality — the one
To end in madness — both in misery.

Prometheus

I

Titan! to whose immortal eyes
    The sufferings of mortality,
    Seen in their sad reality,
Were not as things that gods despise;
What was thy pity's recompense?
A silent suffering, and intense;
The rock, the vulture, and the chain,
All that the proud can feel of pain,
The agony they do not show,
The suffocating sense of woe,
    Which speaks but in its loneliness,
And then is jealous lest the sky
Should have a listener, nor will sigh
    Until its voice is echoless.

II

Titan! to thee the strife was given
    Between the suffering and the will,
    Which torture where they cannot kill;
And the inexorable Heaven,
And the deaf tyranny of Fate,
The ruling principle of Hate,
Which for its pleasure doth create
The things it may annihilate,
Refused thee even the boon to die:
The wretched gift Eternity
Was thine – and thou hast borne it well.
All that the Thunderer wrung from thee
Was but the menace which flung back
On him the torments of thy rack;

The fate thou didst so well foresee,
But would not to appease him tell;
And in thy Silence was his Sentence,
And in his Soul a vain repentance,
And evil dread so ill dissembled,
That in his hand the lightnings trembled.

III

Thy Godlike crime was to be kind,
 To render with thy precepts less
 The sum of human wretchedness,
And strengthen Man with his own mind;
But baffled as thou wert from high,
Still in thy patient energy,
In the endurance, and repulse
 Of thine impenetrable Spirit,
Which Earth and Heaven could not convulse,
 A mighty lesson we inherit:
Thou art a symbol and a sign
 To Mortals of their fate and force;
Like thee, Man is in part divine,
 A troubled stream from a pure source;
And Man in portions can foresee
His own funereal destiny;
His wretchedness, and his resistance,
And his sad unallied existence:
To which his Spirit may oppose
Itself – an equal to all woes –
 And a firm will, and a deep sense,
Which even in torture can descry
 Its own concentered recompense,
Triumphant where it dares defy,
And making Death a Victory.

Storm in the Alps (from *Childe Harold's Pilgrimage*, Canto III)

The sky is changed! – and such a change! Oh night,
And Storm, and Darkness, ye are wondrous strong,
Yet lovely in your strength, as is the light
Of a dark eye in Woman! Far along,
From peak to peak, the rattling crags among
Leaps the live thunder! Not from one lone cloud,
But every mountain now hath found a tongue,
And Jura answers, through her misty shroud,
Back to the joyous Alps, who call to her aloud!

And this is in the night: – Most glorious Night!
Thou wert not sent for slumber! let me be
A sharer in thy fierce and far delight, –
A portion of the tempest and of thee!
How the lit lake shines, a phosphoric sea,
And the big rain comes dancing to the earth!
And now again 'tis black, – and now, the glee
Of the loud hills shakes with its mountain-mirth,
As if they did rejoice o'er a young Earthquake's birth.

Darkness

I had a dream, which was not all a dream.
The bright sun was extinguished, and the stars
Did wander darkling in the eternal space,
Rayless, and pathless, and the icy Earth
Swung blind and blackening in the moonless air;
Morn came and went — and came, and brought no day,
And men forgot their passions in the dread
Of this their desolation; and all hearts
Were chilled into a selfish prayer for light:
And they did live by watchfires — and the thrones,
The palaces of crowned kings — the huts,
The habitations of all things which dwell,
Were burnt for beacons; cities were consumed,
And men were gathered round their blazing homes
To look once more into each other's face;
Happy were those who dwelt within the eye
Of the volcanos, and their mountain-torch:
A fearful hope was all the World contained;
Forests were set on fire — but hour by hour
They fell and faded — and the crackling trunks
Extinguished with a crash — and all was black.
The brows of men by the despairing light
Wore an unearthly aspect, as by fits
The flashes fell upon them; some lay down
And hid their eyes and wept; and some did rest
Their chins upon their clenched hands, and smiled;
And others hurried to and fro, and fed
Their funeral piles with fuel, and looked up
With mad disquietude on the dull sky,
The pall of a past World; and then again

With curses cast them down upon the dust,
And gnashed their teeth and howled: the wild birds
   shrieked,
And, terrified, did flutter on the ground,
And flap their useless wings; the wildest brutes
Came tame and tremulous; and vipers crawled
And twined themselves among the multitude,
Hissing, but stingless – they were slain for food:
And War, which for a moment was no more,
Did glut himself again: – a meal was bought
With blood, and each sate sullenly apart
Gorging himself in gloom: no Love was left;
All earth was but one thought – and that was Death,
Immediate and inglorious; and the pang
Of famine fed upon all entrails – men
Died, and their bones were tombless as their flesh;
The meagre by the meagre were devoured,
Even dogs assailed their masters, all save one,
And he was faithful to a corse, and kept
The birds and beasts and famished men at bay,
Till hunger clung them, or the dropping dead
Lured their lank jaws; himself sought out no food,
But with a piteous and perpetual moan,
And a quick desolate cry, licking the hand
Which answered not with a caress – he died.
The crowd was famished by degrees; but two
Of an enormous city did survive,
And they were enemies: they met beside
The dying embers of an altar-place
Where had been heaped a mass of holy things
For an unholy usage; they raked up,
And shivering scraped with their cold skeleton hands

The feeble ashes, and their feeble breath
Blew for a little life, and made a flame
Which was a mockery; then they lifted up
Their eyes as it grew lighter, and beheld
Each other's aspects – saw, and shrieked, and died –
Even of their mutual hideousness they died,
Unknowing who he was upon whose brow
Famine had written Fiend. The World was void,
The populous and the powerful was a lump,
Seasonless, herbless, treeless, manless, lifeless –
A lump of death – a chaos of hard clay.
The rivers, lakes, and ocean all stood still,
And nothing stirred within their silent depths;
Ships sailorless lay rotting on the sea,
And their masts fell down piecemeal: as they dropped
They slept on the abyss without a surge –
The waves were dead; the tides were in their grave,
The Moon, their mistress, had expired before;
The winds were withered in the stagnant air,
And the clouds perished; Darkness had no need
Of aid from them – She was the Universe.

The Assault (from *The Siege of Corinth*)

The night is past, and shines the sun
As if that morn were a jocund one.
Lightly and brightly breaks away
The Morning from her mantle grey,
And the Noon will look on a sultry day.
Hark to the trump, and the drum,
And the mournful sound of the barbarous horn,
And the flap of the banners, that flit as they're borne,
And the neigh of the steed, and the multitude's hum,
And the clash, and the shout, 'They come! they come!'
The horsetails are plucked from the ground, and the
    sword
From its sheath; and they form, and but wait for the
    word.
Tartar, and Spahi, and Turcoman,
Strike your tents, and throng to the van;
Mount ye, spur ye, skirr the plain,
That the fugitive may flee in vain,
When he breaks from the town; and none escape,
Aged or young, in the Christian shape;
While your fellows on foot, in a fiery mass,
Bloodstain the breach through which they pass.
The steeds are all bridled, and snort to the rein;
Curved is each neck, and flowing each mane;
White is the foam of their champ on the bit:
The spears are uplifted; the matches are lit;
The cannon are pointed, and ready to roar,
And crush the wall they have crumbled before:
Forms in his phalanx each Janizar;
Alp at their head; his right arm is bare,

So is the blade of his scimitar;
The Khan and the Pachas are all at their post;
The Vizier himself at the head of the host.
When the culverin's signal is fired, then on;
Leave not in Corinth a living one –
A priest at her altars, a chief in her halls,
A hearth in her mansions, a stone on her walls.
God and the prophet – Alla Hu!
Up to the skies with that wild halloo!
'There the breach lies for passage, the ladder to scale;
And your hands on your sabres, and how should ye fail?
He who first downs with the red cross may crave
His heart's dearest wish; let him ask it, and have!'
Thus utter'd Coumourgi, the dauntless vizier;
The reply was the brandish of sabre and spear,
And the shout of fierce thousands in joyous ire: –
Silence – hark to the signal – fire!

* * * * *

From the point of encountering blades to the hilt,
Sabres and swords with blood were gilt:
But the rampart is won, and the spoil begun,
And all but the after carnage done.
Shriller shrieks now mingling come
From within the plundered dome:
Hark to the haste of flying feet,
That splash in the blood of the slippery street;
But here and there, where 'vantage ground
Against the foe may still be found,
Desperate groups of twelve or ten
Make a pause, and turn again –

With banded backs against the wall
Fiercely stand, or fighting fall.

There stood an old man — his hairs were white,
But his veteran arm was full of might:
So gallantly bore he the brunt of the fray,
The dead before him, on that day,
In a semicircle lay;
Still he combated unwounded,
Though retreating, unsurrounded.
Many a scar of former fight
Lurk'd beneath his corslet bright;
But of every wound his body bore,
Each and all had been ta'en before:
Though aged, he was so iron of limb,
Few of our youth could cope with him;
And the foes, whom he singly kept at bay,
Outnumbered his thin hairs of silver grey.

* * * * *

Still the old man stood erect,
And Alp's career a moment check'd.
'Yield thee, Minotti; quarter take,
For thine own, thy daughter's sake.'

'Never, renegado, never!
Though the life of thy gift would last for ever.'
'Francesca! — Oh, my promised bride!
Must she too perish by thy pride?'

'She is safe.' – 'Where? where?' – 'In heaven;
From whence thy traitor soul is driven –
Far from thee, and undefiled.'
Grimly then Minotti smiled,
As he saw Alp staggering bow
Before his words, as with a blow.
'Oh God! when died she?' – 'Yesternight –
Nor weep I for her spirit's flight:
None of my pure race shall be
Slaves to Mahomet and thee –
Come on!' – That challenge is in vain –
Alp's already with the slain!

While Minotti's words were wreaking
More revenge in bitter speaking
Than his falchion's point had found
Had the time allow'd to wound,
From within the neighbouring porch
Of a long defended church,
Where the last and desperate few
Would the failing fight renew,
The sharp shot dash'd Alp to the ground.
Ere an eye could view the wound
That crash'd through the brain of the infidel,
Round he spun, and down he fell.

Nature the Consoler (from *Childe Harold's Pilgrimage*, Canto III)

Where rose the mountains, there to him were
    friends;
Where roll'd the ocean, thereon was his home;
Where a blue sky, and glowing clime, extends,
He had the passion and the power to roam;
The desert, forest, cavern, breaker's foam,
Were unto him companionship; they spake
A mutual language, clearer than the tome
Of his land's tongue, which he would oft
    forsake
For Nature's pages glass'd by sunbeams on the lake.

Like the Chaldean, he could watch the stars,
Till he had peopled them with beings bright
As their own beams; and earth, and earth-born
    jars,
And human frailties, were forgotten quite:
Could he have kept his spirit to that flight
He had been happy; but this clay will sink
Its spark immortal, envying it the light
To which it mounts, as if to break the link
That keeps us from yon heaven which woos us to its
    brink.

But in Man's dwellings he became a thing
Restless and worn, and stern and wearisome,
Droop'd as a wild-born falcon with clipt wing,
To whom the boundless air alone were home:
Then came his fit again, which to o'ercome,

As eagerly the barr'd-up bird will beat
His breast and beak against his wiry dome
Till the blood tinge his plumage, so the heat
Of his impeded soul would through his bosom eat.

The Poet and the World (from *Childe Harold's Pilgrimage*, Canto III)

I have not loved the world, nor the world me;
I have not flatter'd its rank breath, nor bow'd
To its idolatries a patient knee, –
Nor coin'd my cheek to smiles, – nor cried aloud
In worship of an echo; in the crowd
They could not deem me one of such; I stood
Among them, but not of them; in a shroud
Of thoughts which were not their thoughts, and still
    could,
Had I not filed my mind, which thus itself subdued.

I have not loved the world, nor the world me, –
But let us part fair foes; I do believe,
Though I have found them not, that there may be
Words which are things, – hopes which will not
    deceive,
And virtues which are merciful, nor weave
Snares for the failing: I would also deem
O'er others' griefs that some sincerely grieve;
That two, or one, are almost what they seem, –
That goodness is no name, and happiness no dream.

Ruins to Ruins (from *Childe Harold's Pilgrimage*, Canto IV)

Oh Time! the beautifier of the dead,
Adorner of the ruin, comforter
And only healer when the heart hath bled –
Time! the corrector where our judgments err,
The test of truth, love, – sole philosopher,
For all beside are sophists, from thy thrift,
Which never loses though it doth defer –
Time, the avenger! unto thee I lift
My hands, and eyes, and heart, and crave of thee a gift:

Amidst this wreck, where thou hast made a shrine
And temple more divinely desolate,
Among thy mightier offerings here are mine,
Ruins of years – though few, yet full of fate: –
If thou hast ever seen me too elate,
Hear me not; but if calmly I have borne
Good, and reserved my pride against the hate
Which shall not whelm me, let me not have worn
This iron in my soul in vain – shall *they* not mourn?

Epistle to Augusta

I

My Sister! my sweet Sister! if a name
Dearer and purer were, it should be thine.
Mountains and seas divide us, but I claim
No tears, but tenderness to answer mine:
Go where I will, to me thou art the same –
A loved regret which I would not resign.
There yet are two things in my destiny, –
A world to roam through, and a home with thee.

II

The first were nothing – had I still the last,
It were the haven of my happiness;
But other claims and other ties thou hast,
And mine is not the wish to make them less.
A strange doom is thy father's son's, and past
Recalling, as it lies beyond redress;
Reversed for him our grandsire's fate of yore, –
He had no rest at sea, nor I on shore.

III

If my inheritance of storms hath been
In other elements, and on the rocks
Of perils, overlooked or unforeseen,
I have sustained my share of worldly shocks,
The fault was mine; nor do I seek to screen
My errors with defensive paradox;
I have been cunning in mine overthrow,
The careful pilot of my proper woe.

IV

Mine were my faults, and mine be their
    reward.
My whole life was a contest, since the day
That gave me being, gave me that which marred
The gift, — a fate, or will, that walked astray;
And I at times have found the struggle hard,
And thought of shaking off my bonds of clay:
But now I fain would for a time survive,
If but to see what next can well arrive.

V

Kingdoms and Empires in my little day
I have outlived, and yet I am not old;
And when I look on this, the petty spray
Of my own years of trouble, which have
    rolled
Like a wild bay of breakers, melts away:
Something — I know not what — does still uphold
A spirit of slight patience; — not in vain,
Even for its own sake, do we purchase Pain.

VI

Perhaps the workings of defiance stir
Within me — or, perhaps, a cold despair
Brought on when ills habitually recur, —
Perhaps a kinder clime, or purer air,
(For even to this may change of soul refer,
And with light armour we may learn to bear,)
Have taught me a strange quiet, which was not
The chief companion of a calmer lot.

VII

I feel almost at times as I have felt
In happy childhood; trees, and flowers, and brooks,
Which do remember me of where I dwelt,
Ere my young mind was sacrificed to books,
Come as of yore upon me, and can melt
My heart with recognition of their looks;
And even at moments I could think I see
Some living thing to love — but none like thee.

VIII

Here are the Alpine landscapes which create
A fund for contemplation; — to admire
Is a brief feeling of a trivial date;
But something worthier do such scenes inspire:
Here to be lonely is not desolate,
For much I view which I could most desire,
And, above all, a Lake I can behold
Lovelier, not dearer, than our own of old.

IX

Oh that thou wert but with me! — but I
    grow
The fool of my own wishes, and forget
The solitude which I have vaunted so
Has lost its praise in this but one regret;
There may be others which I less may show; —
I am not of the plaintive mood, and yet
I feel an ebb in my philosophy,
And the tide rising in my altered eye.

X

I did remind thee of our own dear Lake,
By the old Hall which may be mine no more.
Leman's is fair; but think not I forsake
The sweet remembrance of a dearer shore:
Sad havoc Time must with my memory make,
Ere that or thou can fade these eyes before;
Though, like all things which I have loved, they are
Resigned for ever, or divided far.

XI

The world is all before me; I but ask
Of Nature that with which she will comply –
It is but in her Summer's sun to bask,
To mingle with the quiet of her sky,
To see her gentle face without a mask,
And never gaze on it with apathy.
She was my early friend, and now shall be
My sister – till I look again on thee.

XII

I can reduce all feelings but this one;
And that I would not; – for at length I see
Such scenes as those wherein my life begun –
The earliest – even the only paths for me –
Had I but sooner learnt the crowd to shun,
I had been better than I now can be;
The Passions which have torn me would have
    slept;
I had not suffered, and thou hadst not wept.

XIII

With false Ambition what had I to do?
Little with Love, and least of all with Fame;
And yet they came unsought, and with me grew,
And made me all which they can make – a Name.
Yet this was not the end I did pursue;
Surely I once beheld a nobler aim.
But all is over – I am one the more
To baffled millions which have gone before.

XIV

And for the future, this world's future may
From me demand but little of my care;
I have outlived myself by many a day;
Having survived so many things that were;
My years have been no slumber, but the prey
Of ceaseless vigils; for I had the share
Of life which might have filled a century,
Before its fourth in time had passed me by.

XV

And for the remnant which may be to come
I am content; and for the past I feel
Not thankless, – for within the crowded sum
Of struggles, Happiness at times would steal,
And for the present, I would not benumb
My feelings farther. – Nor shall I conceal
That with all this I still can look around,
And worship Nature with a thought profound.

XVI

For thee, my own sweet sister, in thy heart
I know myself secure, as thou in mine;
We were and are – I am, even as thou art –
Beings who ne'er each other can resign;
It is the same, together or apart,
From Life's commencement to its slow decline
We are entwined – let Death come slow or fast,
The tie which bound the first endures the last!

Stanzas to Augusta

Though the day of my destiny's over,
    And the star of my fate hath declined,
Thy soft heart refused to discover
    The faults which so many could find;
Though thy soul with my grief was acquainted,
    It shrunk not to share it with me,
And the love which my spirit hath painted
    It never hath found but in thee.

Then when nature around me is smiling,
    The last smile which answers to mine,
I do not believe it beguiling,
    Because it reminds me of thine;
And when winds are at war with the ocean,
    As the breasts I believed in with me,
If their billows excite an emotion,
    It is that they bear me from thee.

Though the rock of my last hope is shiver'd,
    And its fragments are sunk in the wave,
Though I feel that my soul is deliver'd
    To pain – it shall not be its slave.
There is many a pang to pursue me:
    They may crush, but they shall not contemn –
They may torture, but shall not subdue me –
    'Tis of thee that I think – not of them.

Though human, thou didst not deceive me,
    Though woman, thou didst not forsake,
Though loved, thou forborest to grieve me,

Though slander'd, thou never could'st shake, —
Though trusted, thou didst not disclaim me,
    Though parted, it was not to fly,
Though watchful, 'twas not to defame me,
    Nor, mute, that the world might belie.

Yet I blame not the world, nor despise it,
    Nor the war of the many with one —
If my soul was not fitted to prize it,
    'Twas folly not sooner to shun:
And if dearly that error hath cost me,
    And more than I once could foresee,
I have found that, whatever it lost me,
    It could not deprive me of thee.

From the wreck of the past, which hath perish'd,
    Thus much I at least may recall,
It hath taught me that what I most cherish'd
    Deserved to be dearest of all:
In the desert a fountain is springing,
    In the wide waste there still is a tree,
And a bird in the solitude singing,
    Which speaks to my spirit of thee.

Thou Art Not False, but Thou Art Fickle

I

Thou art not false, but thou art fickle,
To those thyself so fondly sought;
The tears that thou hast forced to trickle
Are doubly bitter from that thought:
'Tis this which breaks the heart thou grievest,
Too well thou lov'st — too soon thou leavest.

II

The wholly false the heart despises,
And spurns deceiver and deceit;
But she who not a thought disguises,
Whose love is as sincere as sweet, —
When she can change who loved so truly,
It feels what mine has felt so newly.

III

To dream of joy and wake to sorrow
Is doomed to all who love or live;
And if, when conscious on the morrow,
We scarce our Fancy can forgive,
That cheated us in slumber only,
To leave the waking soul more lonely,

IV

What must they feel whom no false vision
But truest, tenderest Passion warmed?
Sincere, but swift in sad transition:
As if a dream alone had charmed?

Ah! sure such *grief* is *Fancy's* scheming,
And all thy *Change* can be but *dreaming*!

So, We'll Go No More A Roving

I

So, we'll go no more a roving
    So late into the night,
Though the heart be still as loving,
    And the moon be still as bright.

II

For the sword outwears its sheath,
    And the soul wears out the breast,
And the heart must pause to breathe,
    And love itself have rest.

III

Though the night was made for loving,
    And the day returns too soon,
Yet we'll go no more a roving
    By the light of the moon.

Epistle from Mr Murray to Dr Polidori

Dear Doctor, I have read your play,
Which is a good one in its way, –
Purges the eyes, and moves the bowels,
And drenches handkerchiefs like towels
With tears, that, in a flux of grief,
Afford hysterical relief
To shattered nerves and quickened pulses,
Which your catastrophe convulses.

  I like your moral and machinery;
Your plot, too, has such scope for Scenery!
Your dialogue is apt and smart;
The play's concoction full of art;
Your hero raves, your heroine cries
All stab, and every body dies.
In short, your tragedy would be
The very thing to hear and see:
And for a piece of publication,
If I decline on this occasion,
It is not that I am not sensible
To merits in themselves ostensible,
But – and I grieve to speak it – plays
Are drugs – mere drugs, Sir – now-a-days.
I had a heavy loss by *Manuel* –
Too lucky if it prove not annual, –
And Sotheby, with his *Orestes*,
(Which, by the way, the old Bore's best is,)
Has lain so very long on hand,
That I despair of all demand;
I've advertised, but see my books,
Or only watch my Shopman's looks; –

Still Ivan, Ina, and such lumber,
My back-shop glut, my shelves encumber.

  There's Byron too, who once did better,
Has sent me, folded in a letter,
A sort of – it's no more a drama
Than Darnley, Ivan, or Kehama;
So altered since last year his pen is,
I think he's lost his wits at Venice.
Or drained his brains away as Stallion
To some dark-eyed and warm Italian;
In short, Sir, what with one and t'other,
I dare not venture on another.
I write in haste; excuse each blunder;
The Coaches through the street so thunder!
My room's so full – we've Gifford here
Reading MS., with Hookham Frere,
Pronouncing on the nouns and particles,
Of some of our forthcoming Articles.

  The Quarterly – Ah, Sir, if you
Had but the Genius to review! –
A smart Critique upon St. Helena,
Or if you only would but tell in a
Short compass what – but to resume;
As I was saying, Sir, the Room –
The Room's so full of wits and bards,
Crabbes, Campbells, Crokers, Freres, and Wards
And others, neither bards nor wits:
My humble tenement admits
All persons in the dress of Gent.,
From Mr Hammond to Dog Dent.

  A party dines with me today,
All clever men, who make their way:

Crabbe, Malcolm, Hamilton, and Chantrey,
Are all partakers of my pantry.
They're at this moment in discussion
On poor De Staël's late dissolution.
Her book, they say, was in advance –
Pray Heaven, she tell the truth of France!
'Tis said she certainly was married
To Rocca, and had twice miscarried,
No – not miscarried, I opine, –
But brought to bed at forty-nine.
Some say she died a Papist; some
Are of opinion that's a Hum;
I don't know that – the fellows Schlegel,
Are very likely to inveigle
A dying person in compunction
To try the extremity of Unction.
But peace be with her! for a woman
Her talents surely were uncommon,
Her Publisher (and Public too)
The hour of her demise may rue –
For never more within his shop he –
Pray – Was not she interred at Coppet?
Thus run our time and tongues away; –
But, to return, Sir, to your play:
Sorry, Sir, but I cannot deal,
Unless 'twere acted by O'Neill.
My hands are full – my head so busy,
I'm almost dead – and always dizzy;
And so, with endless truth and hurry,
Dear Doctor, I am yours,

JOHN MURRAY.

Epistle to Mr Murray

I

My dear Mr Murray,
You're in a damned hurry
    To set up this ultimate Canto;
But (if they don't rob us)
You'll see Mr Hobhouse
    Will bring it safe in his portmanteau.

II

For the Journal you hint of,
As ready to print off,
    No doubt you do right to commend it;
But as yet I have writ off
The devil a bit of
    Our 'Beppo': – when copied, I'll send it.

III

In the mean time you've 'Galley'
Whose verses all tally,
    Perhaps you may say he's a Ninny,
But if you abashed are
Because of *Alashtar*,
    He'll piddle another *Phrosine*.

IV

Then you've Sotheby's Tour, –
No great things, to be sure, –
    You could hardly begin with a less work;
For the pompous rascallion,

Who don't speak Italian
    Nor French, must have scribbled by guess-work.

V

No doubt he's a rare man
Without knowing German
    Translating his way up Parnassus,
And now still absurder
He meditates Murder
    As you'll see in the trash he calls *Tasso*'s.

VI

But you've others his betters
The real men of letters
    Your Orators – Critics – and Wits –
And I'll bet that your Journal
(Pray is it diurnal?)
    Will pay with your luckiest hits.

VII

You can make any loss up
With 'Spence' and his gossip,
    A work which must surely succeed;
Then Queen Mary's Epistle-craft,
With the new 'Fytte' of 'Whistlecraft,'
    Must make people purchase and read.

VIII

Then you've General Gordon,
Who girded his sword on,
    To serve with a Muscovite Master,
And help him to polish

A nation so owlish,
      They thought shaving their beards a disaster.

IX

For the man, '*poor and shrewd*',
With whom you'd conclude
      A compact without more delay,
Perhaps some such pen is
Still extant in Venice;
      But please, Sir, to mention *your pay*.

X

Now tell me some news
Of your friends and the Muse,
      Of the Bar, or the Gown, or the House,
From Canning, the tall wit,
To Wilmot, the small wit,
      Ward's creeping Companion and *Louse*,

XI

Who's so damnably bit
With fashion and Wit,
      That he crawls on the surface like Vermin,
But an Insect in both, –
By his Intellect's growth,
      Of what size you may quickly determine.

The Coliseum (from *Childe Harold's Pilgrimage*, Canto IV)

Arches on arches! as it were that Rome,
Collecting the chief trophies of her line,
Would build up all her triumphs in one dome,
Her Coliseum stands; the moonbeams shine
As 'twere its natural torches, for divine
Should be the light which streams here, to illume
This long-explored, but still exhaustless, mine
Of contemplation; and the azure gloom
Of an Italian night, where the deep skies assume

Hues which have words, and speak to ye of
 heaven,
Floats o'er this vast and wondrous monument,
And shadows forth its glory. There is given
Unto the things of earth, which Time hath bent,
A spirit's feeling, and where he hath leant
His hand, but broke his scythe, there is a power
And magic in the ruined battlement,
For which the palace of the present hour
Must yield its pomp, and wait till ages are its dower.

* * * * *

And here the buzz of eager nations ran,
In murmured pity, or loud-roared applause,
As man was slaughtered by his fellow man.
And wherefore slaughtered? wherefore, but because
Such were the bloody Circus' genial laws,
And the imperial pleasure. – Wherefore not?

What matters where we fall to fill the maws
Of worms – on battle-plains or listed spot?
Both are but theatres where the chief actors rot.

I see before me the Gladiator lie:
He leans upon his hand – his manly brow
Consents to death, but conquers agony,
And his drooped head sinks gradually low –
And through his side the last drops, ebbing slow
From the red gash, fall heavy, one by one,
Like the first of a thunder-shower; and now
The arena swims around him – he is gone,
Ere ceased the inhuman shout which hailed the wretch
   who won.

He heard it, but he heeded not – his eyes
Were with his heart, and that was far away;
He recked not of the life he lost, nor prize,
But where his rude hut by the Danube lay,
There were his young barbarians all at play,
There was their Dacian mother – he, their sire,
Butchered to make a Roman holiday –
All this rushed with his blood. – Shall he expire
And unavenged? Arise! ye Goths, and glut your ire!

But here, where Murder breathed her bloody steam;
And here, where buzzing nations choked the ways,
And roared or murmured like a mountain stream
Dashing or winding as its torrent strays;
Here, where the Roman million's blame or praise
Was Death or Life, the playthings of a crowd,
My voice sounds much – and fall the stars' faintrays

On the arena void, seats crushed, walls bowed,
And galleries, where my steps seem echoes strangely loud.

A Ruin — yet what Ruin! from its mass
Walls, palaces, half-cities, have been reared;
Yet oft the enormous skeleton ye pass,
And marvel where the spoil could have appeared.
Hath it indeed been plundered, or but cleared?
Alas! developed, opens the decay,
When the colossal fabric's form is neared:
It will not bear the brightness of the day,
Which streams too much on all years, man, have reft
away.

But when the rising moon begins to climb
Its topmost arch, and gently pauses there;
When the stars twinkle through the loops of time,
And the low night-breeze waves along the air
The garland-forest, which the grey walls wear,
Like laurels on the bald first Cæsar's head;
When the light shines serene but doth not glare —
Then in this magic circle raise the dead:
Heroes have trod this spot — 'tis on their dust ye tread.

'While stands the Coliseum, Rome shall stand;
When falls the Coliseum, Rome shall fall;
And when Rome falls — the World.' From our own
land
Thus spake the pilgrims o'er this mighty wall
In Saxon times, which we are wont to call
Ancient; and these three mortal things are still
On their foundations, and unaltered all;

Rome and her Ruin past Redemption's skill,
The World, the same wide den — of thieves, or what ye
will.

Nature to the Last (from *Childe Harold's Pilgrimage*, Canto IV)

My Pilgrim's shrine is won,
And he and I must part, – so let it be, –
His task and mine alike are nearly done;
Yet once more let us look upon the Sea;
The Midland Ocean breaks on him and me,
And from the Alban Mount we now behold
Our friend of youth, that Ocean, which when we
Beheld it last by Calpe's rock unfold
Those waves, we followed on till the dark Euxine rolled

Upon the blue Symplegades: long years –
Long, though not very many, since have done
Their work on both; some suffering and some tears
Have left us nearly where we had begun:
Yet not in vain our mortal race hath run,
We have had our reward – and it is here;
That we can yet feel gladden'd by the sun,
And reap from earth, sea, joy almost as dear
As if there were no man to trouble what is clear.

Oh! that the Desert were my dwelling place,
With one fair Spirit for my minister,
That I might all forget the human race,
And, hating no one, love but only her!
Ye Elements! – in whose ennobling stir
I feel myself exalted – Can ye not
Accord me such a Being? Do I err
In deeming such inhabit many a spot?
Though with them to converse can rarely be our lot.

There is a pleasure in the pathless woods,
There is a rapture on the lonely shore,
There is society, where none intrudes,
By the deep Sea, and Music in its roar.
I love not Man the less, but Nature more,
From these our interviews, in which I steal
From all I may be, or have been before,
To mingle with the Universe, and feel
What I can ne'er express, yet can not all conceal.

Roll on, thou deep and dark blue Ocean – roll!
Ten thousand fleets sweep over thee in vain;
Man marks the earth with ruin – his control
Stops with the shore; – upon the watery plain
The wrecks are all thy deed, nor doth remain
A shadow of man's ravage, save his own,
When, for a moment, like a drop of rain,
He sinks into thy depths with bubbling
    groan,
Without a grave, unknell'd, uncoffin'd, and unknown.

His steps are not upon thy paths, – thy fields
Are not a spoil for him, – thou dost arise
And shake him from thee; the vile strength he
    wields
For Earth's destruction thou dost all despise,
Spurning him from thy bosom to the skies,
And send'st him, shivering in thy playful
    spray
And howling, to his Gods, where haply lies
His petty hope in some near port or bay,
And dashest him again to Earth: – there let him lay.

The armaments which thunderstrike the walls
Of rock-built cities, bidding nations quake,
And Monarchs tremble in their Capitals,
The oak Leviathans, whose huge ribs make
Their clay creator the vain title take
Of Lord of thee, and Arbiter of War;
These are thy toys, and, as the snowy flake,
They melt into thy yeast of waves, which mar
Alike the Armada's pride, or spoils of Trafalgar.

Thy shores are empires, changed in all save thee —
Assyria, Greece, Rome, Carthage, what are they?
Thy waters wasted them while they were free,
And many a tyrant since; their shores obey
The stranger, slave, or savage; their decay
Has dried up realms to deserts: — not so thou,
Unchangeable save to thy wild waves' play —
Time writes no wrinkle on thine azure brow —
Such as Creation's dawn beheld, thou rollest now.

Thou glorious mirror, where the Almighty's form
Glasses itself in tempests; in all time,
Calm or convulsed — in breeze, or gale, or storm,
Icing the Pole, or in the torrid clime
Dark-heaving; — boundless, endless, and sublime —
The image of Eternity — the throne
Of the Invisible, even from out thy slime
The monsters of the deep are made; each Zone
Obeys thee; thou goest forth, dread, fathomless, alone.

And I have loved thee, Ocean! and my joy
Of youthful sports was on thy breast to be

Born, like thy bubbles, onward: from a boy
I wanton'd with thy breakers – they to me
Were a delight; and if the freshening sea
Made them a terror – 'twas a pleasing fear,
For I was as it were a child of thee,
And trusted to thy billows far and near,
And laid my hand upon thy mane – as I do here.

Dedication (from *Don Juan*)

Difficile est proprie communia dicere. HOR. *Epist. ad Pison*

I

Bob Southey! You're a poet — Poet-laureate,
    And representative of all the race;
Although 'tis true that you turn'd out a Tory at
    Last — yours has lately been a common case;
And now, my Epic Renegade! what are ye at?
    With all the Lakers, in and out of place?
A nest of tuneful persons, to my eye
Like 'four and twenty Blackbirds in a pye;

II

'Which pye being open'd they began to sing'
    (This old song and new simile holds good)
'A dainty dish to set before the King,'
    Or Regent, who admires such kind of food;
And Coleridge, too, has lately taken wing,
    But like a hawk encumber'd with his hood,
Explaining Metaphysics to the nation —
I wish he would explain his Explanation.

III

You, Bob! are rather insolent, you know,
    At being disappointed in your wish
To supersede all warblers here below,
    And be the only Blackbird in the dish;
And then you overstrain yourself, or so,
    And tumble downward like the flying fish

Gasping on deck, because you soar too high, Bob,
And fall, for lack of moisture quite a-dry, Bob!

IV

And Wordsworth, in a rather long 'Excursion'
     (I think the quarto holds five hundred pages),
Has given a sample from the vasty version
     Of his new system to perplex the sages;
'Tis poetry — at least by his assertion,
     And may appear so when the dog-star
        rages —
And he who understands it would be able
To add a story to the Tower of Babel.

V

You — Gentlemen! by dint of long seclusion
     From better company, have kept your own
At Keswick, and, through still continu'd fusion
     Of one another's minds, at last have grown
To deem as a most logical conclusion,
     That Poesy has wreaths for you alone;
There is a narrowness in such a notion,
Which makes me wish you'd change your lakes for
   Ocean.

VI

I would not imitate the petty thought,
     Nor coin my self-love to so base a vice,
For all the glory your conversion brought,
     Since gold alone should not have been its price.
You have your salary; was't for that you wrought?

And Wordsworth has his place in the Excise.
You're shabby fellows – true – but poets still,
And duly seated on the Immortal Hill.

VII

Your bays may hide the baldness of your brows –
    Perhaps some virtuous blushes – let them go –
To you I envy neither fruit nor boughs –
    And for the fame you would engross below,
The field is universal, and allows
    Scope to all such as feel the inherent glow:
Scott, Rogers, Campbell, Moore and Crabbe, will try
'Gainst you the question with posterity.

VIII

For me, who, wandering with pedestrian Muses,
    Contend not with you on the winged steed,
I wish your fate may yield ye, when she chooses,
    The fame you envy, and the skill you need;
And, recollect, a poet nothing loses
    In giving to his brethren their full meed
Of merit, and complaint of present days
Is not the certain path to future praise.

IX

He that reserves his laurels for posterity
    (Who does not often claim the bright reversion?)
Has generally no great crop to spare it, he
    Being only injur'd by his own assertion;
And although here and there some glorious rarity
    Arise, like Titan from the sea's immersion,

The major part of such appellants go
To — God knows where — for no one else can know.

X

If, fallen in evil days on evil tongues,
  Milton appeal'd to the Avenger, Time,
If Time, the Avenger, execrates his wrongs,
  And makes the word 'Miltonic' mean 'sublime,'
He deign'd not to belie his soul in songs,
  Nor turn his very talent to a crime —
He did not loathe the Sire to laud the Son,
But clos'd the tyrant-hater he begun.

XI

Think'st thou, could he — the blind Old Man — arise
  Like Samuel from the grave, to freeze once
   more
The blood of monarchs with his prophecies,
  Or be alive again — again all hoar
With time and trials, and those helpless eyes,
  And heartless daughters — worn — and pale — and
   poor;
Would he adore a sultan? he obey
The intellectual eunuch Castlereagh?

XII

Cold-blooded, smooth-fac'd, placid miscreant!
  Dabbling its sleek young hands in Erin's gore,
And thus for wider carnage taught to pant,
  Transferr'd to gorge upon a sister-shore,
The vulgarest tool that Tyranny could want,

With just enough of talent, and no more,
To lengthen fetters by another fix'd,
And offer poison long already mix'd.

XIII

An orator of such set trash of phrase
    Ineffably – legitimately vile,
That even its grossest flatterers dare not praise,
    Nor foes – all nations – condescend to smile,
Not even a sprightly blunder's spark can blaze
    From that Ixion grindstone's ceaseless toil,
That turns and turns to give the world a notion
Of endless torments and perpetual motion.

XIV

A bungler even in its disgusting trade,
    And botching, patching, leaving still behind
Something of which its masters are afraid,
    States to be curb'd, and thoughts to be
        confined,
Conspiracy or Congress to be made –
    Cobbling at manacles for all mankind –
A tinkering slavemaker, who mends old chains,
With God and Man's abhorrence for its gains.

XV

If we may judge of matter by the mind,
    Emasculated to the marrow, It
Hath but two objects – how to serve, and bind,
    Deeming the chain it wears even men may
        fit;
Eutropius of its many masters – blind

To worth as freedom, wisdom as to wit,
Fearless — because no feeling dwells in ice,
Its very courage stagnates to a vice.

XVI

Where shall I turn me not to view its bonds?
For I will never feel them — Italy!
Thy late reviving Roman soul desponds
Beneath the lie this State-thing breathed o'er thee;
Thy clanking chain, and Erin's yet green wounds,
Have voices — tongues to cry aloud for me.
Europe has slaves — allies — kings — armies still,
And Southey lives to sing them very ill.

XVII

Meantime — Sir Laureate — I proceed to dedicate
In honest, simple verse, this song to you;
And, if in flattering strains I do not predicate,
'Tis that I still retain my 'buff and blue';
My politics, as yet, are all to educate;
Apostasy's so fashionable, too,
To keep one creed's a task grown quite Herculean;
Is it not so, my Tory, ultra-Julian?

The Wreck (from *Don Juan*, Canto II)

Then rose from sea to sky the wild farewell,
Then shriek'd the timid, and stood still the brave,
Then some leap'd overboard with dreadful yell,
    As eager to anticipate their grave;
And the sea yawn'd around her like a hell,
    And down she suck'd with her the whirling wave,
Like one who grapples with his enemy,
And strives to strangle him before he die.

And first one universal shriek there rush'd,
    Louder than the loud ocean, like a crash
Of echoing thunder; and then all was hush'd,
    Save the wild wind and the remorseless dash
Of billows; but at intervals there gush'd,
    Accompanied with a convulsive splash,
A solitary shriek, the bubbling cry
Of some strong swimmer in his agony.

Mazeppa's Ride (from *Mazeppa*)

'Bring forth the horse!' – the horse was brought;
      In truth he was a noble steed,
      A Tartar of the Ukraine breed,
Who look'd as though the speed of thought
Were in his limbs; but he was wild,
      Wild as the wild deer, and untaught,
With spur and bridle undefiled –
      'Twas but a day he had been caught;
And snorting, with erected mane,
And struggling fiercely, but in vain,
In the full foam of wrath and dread
To me the desert-born was led:
They bound me on, that menial throng,
Upon his back with many a thong;
Then loosed him with a sudden lash –
Away! – away! – and on we dash! –
Torrents less rapid and less rash.

'Away! – away! – My breath was gone –
I saw not where he hurried on:
'Twas scarcely yet the break of day,
And on he foam'd – away! – away! –
The last of human sounds which rose,
As I was darted from my foes,
Was the wild shout of savage laughter,
Which on the wind came roaring after
A moment from that rabble rout:
With sudden wrath I wrench'd my head,
      And snapp'd the cord, which to the mane
      Had bound my neck in lieu of rein,

And, writhing half my form about,
Howl'd back my curse; but 'midst the tread,
The thunder of my courser's speed,
Perchance they did not hear nor heed:
It vexes me – for I would fain
Have paid their insult back again.
I paid it well in after days:
There is not of that castle gate,
Its drawbridge and portcullis' weight,
Stone, bar, moat, bridge, or barrier left;
Nor of its fields a blade of grass,
    Save what grows on a ridge of wall,
    Where stood the hearth-stone of the hall;
And many a time ye there might pass,
Nor dream that e'er that fortress was:
I saw its turrets in a blaze,
Their crackling battlements all cleft,
    And the hot lead pour down like rain
From off the scorch'd and blackening roof,
Whose thickness was not vengeance-proof.
    They little thought that day of pain,
When launch'd as on the lightning's flash,
They bade me to destruction dash,
    That one day I should come again,
With twice five thousand horse, to thank
    The Count for his uncourteous ride.
They play'd me then a bitter prank,
    When, with the wild horse for my guide,
They bound me to his foaming flank:
At length I play'd them one as frank –
For time at last sets all things even –
    And if we do but watch the hour,

There never yet was human power
Which could evade, if unforgiven,
The patient search and vigil long
Of him who treasures up a wrong.

'Away, away, my steed and I,
     Upon the pinions of the wind,
     All human dwellings left behind;
We sped like meteors through the sky,
When with its crackling sound the night
Is chequer'd with the northern light:
Town – village – none were on our track,
     But a wild plain of far extent,
And bounded by a forest black;
     And, save the scarce seen battlement
On distant heights of some strong hold,
Against the Tartars built of old,
No trace of man. The year before
A Turkish army had march'd o'er;
And where the Spahi's hoof hath trod,
The verdure flies the bloody sod: –
The sky was dull, and dim, and grey,
     And a low breeze crept moaning by –
     I could have answer'd with a sigh –
But fast we fled, away, away –
And I could neither sigh nor pray;
And my cold sweat-drops fell like rain
Upon the courser's bristling mane;
But, snorting still with rage and fear,
He flew upon his far career:
At times I almost thought, indeed,
He must have slacken'd in his speed;

But no – my bound and slender frame
    Was nothing to his angry might,
And merely like a spur became:
Each motion which I made to free
My swoln limbs from their agony
    Increased his fury and affright:
I tried my voice, – 'twas faint and low,
But yet he swerved as from a blow;
And, starting to each accent, sprang
As from a sudden trumpet's clang:
Meantime my cords were wet with gore,
Which, oozing through my limbs, ran o'er;
And in my tongue the thirst became
A something fierier far than flame.

'We near'd the wild wood – 'twas so wide,
I saw no bounds on either side;
'Twas studded with old sturdy trees,
That bent not to the roughest breeze
Which howls down from Siberia's waste,
And strips the forest in its haste, –
But these were few, and far between
Set thick with shrubs more young and green,
Luxuriant with their annual leaves,
Ere strown by those autumnal eves
That nip the forest's foliage dead,
Discolour'd with a lifeless red,
Which stands thereon like stiffen'd gore
Upon the slain when battle's o'er,
And some long winter's night hath shed
Its frost o'er every tombless head,
So cold and stark the raven's beak

May peck unpierced each frozen cheek:
'Twas a wild waste of underwood,
And here and there a chestnut stood,
The strong oak, and the hardy pine;
    But far apart – and well it were,
Or else a different lot were mine –
    The boughs gave way, and did not tear
    My limbs; and I found strength to bear
My wounds, already scarr'd with cold –
My bonds forbade to loose my hold.
We rustled through the leaves like wind,
Left shrubs, and trees, and wolves behind;
By night I heard them on the track,
Their troop came hard upon our back,
With their long gallop, which can tire
The hound's deep hate, and hunter's fire:
Where'er we flew they follow'd on,
Nor left us with the morning sun;
Behind I saw them, scarce a rood,
At day-break winding through the wood,
And through the night had heard their feet
Their stealing, rustling step repeat.
Oh! how I wish'd for spear or sword,
At least to die amidst the horde,
And perish – if it must be so –
At bay, destroying many a foe.
When first my courser's race begun,
I wish'd the goal already won;
But now I doubted strength and speed.
Vain doubt! his swift and savage breed
Had nerved him like the mountain-roe;
Nor faster falls the blinding snow

Which whelms the peasant near the door
Whose threshold he shall cross no more,
Bewilder'd with the dazzling blast,
Than through the forest-paths he past –
Untired, untamed, and worse than wild;
All furious as a favour'd child
Balk'd of its wish; or fiercer still –
A woman piqued – who has her will.

'The wood was past; 'twas more than noon,
But chill the air, although in June;
Or it might be my veins ran cold –
Prolong'd endurance tames the bold;
And I was then not what I seem,
But headlong as a wintry stream,
And wore my feelings out before
I well could count their causes o'er;
And what with fury, fear, and wrath,
The tortures which beset my path,
Cold, hunger, sorrow, shame, distress,
Thus bound in nature's nakedness;
Sprung from a race whose rising blood
When stirr'd beyond its calmer mood,
And trodden hard upon, is like
The rattle-snake's, in act to strike,
What marvel if this worn-out trunk
Beneath its woes a moment sunk?
The earth gave way, the skies roll'd round,
I seem'd to sink upon the ground;
But err'd, for I was fastly bound.
My heart turn'd sick, my brain grew sore,
And throbb'd awhile, then beat no more:

The skies spun like a mighty wheel;
I saw the trees like drunkards reel,
And a slight flash sprang o'er my eyes,
Which saw no farther: he who dies
Can die no more than then I died.
O'ertortured by that ghastly ride,
I felt the blackness come and go,
        And strove to wake; but could not make
My senses climb up from below:
I felt as on a plank at sea,
When all the waves that dash o'er thee,
At the same time upheave and whelm,
And hurl thee towards a desert realm.
My undulating life was as
The fancied lights that flitting pass
Our shut eyes in deep midnight, when
Fever begins upon the brain;
But soon it pass'd, with little pain,
        But a confusion worse than such:
        I own that I should deem it much,
Dying, to feel the same again;
And yet I do suppose we must
Feel far more ere we turn to dust:
No matter; I have bared my brow
Full in Death's face – before – and now.

'My thoughts came back; where was I? Cold,
        And numb, and giddy: pulse by pulse
Life reassumed its lingering hold,
And throb by throb; till grown a pang
        Which for a moment would convulse,
        My blood reflow'd, though thick and chill;

My ear with uncooth noises rang,

    My heart began once more to thrill;
My sight return'd, though dim; alas!
And thicken'd, as it were, with glass.
Methought the dash of waves was nigh;
There was a gleam too of the sky,
Studded with stars; – it is no dream;
The wild horse swims the wilder stream!
The bright broad river's gushing tide
Sweeps, winding onward, far and wide,
And we are half-way, struggling o'er
To yon unknown and silent shore.
The waters broke my hollow trance,
And with a temporary strength

    My stiffen'd limbs were rebaptized.
My courser's broad breast proudly braves,
And dashes off the ascending waves,
And onward we advance!
We reach the slippery shore at length,

    A haven I but little prized,
For all behind was dark and drear,
And all before was night and fear.
How many hours of night or day
In those suspended pangs I lay,
I could not tell; I scarcely knew
If this were human breath I drew.

'With glossy skin, and dripping mane,

    And reeling limbs, and reeking flank,
The wild steed's sinewy nerves still strain

    Up the repelling bank.
We gain the top: a boundless plain

Spreads through the shadow of the night,
    And onward, onward, onward, seems,
    Like precipices in our dreams,
To stretch beyond the sight;
And here and there a speck of white,
    Or scatter'd spot of dusky green,
In masses broke into the light,
As rose the moon upon my right.
    But nought distinctly seen
In the dim waste would indicate
The omen of a cottage gate;
No twinkling taper from afar
Stood like a hospitable star;
Not even an ignis-fatuus rose
To make him merry with my woes:
    That very cheat had cheer'd me then!
Although detected, welcome still,
Reminding me, through every ill,
    Of the abodes of men.

'Onward we went – but slack and slow;
    His savage force at length o'erspent,
The drooping courser, faint and low,
    All feebly foaming went.
A sickly infant had had power
To guide him forward in that hour;
    But useless all to me.
His new-born tameness nought avail'd,
My limbs were bound; my force had fail'd,
    Perchance, had they been free.
With feeble effort still I tried
To rend the bonds so starkly tied –

But still it was in vain;
My limbs were only wrung the more,
And soon the idle strife gave o'er,
        Which but prolong'd their pain.
The dizzy race seem'd almost done,
Although no goal was nearly won:
Some streaks announced the coming sun –
        How slow, alas! he came!
Methought that mist of dawning grey
Would never dapple into day;
How heavily it roll'd away –
        Before the eastern flame
Rose crimson, and deposed the stars,
And call'd the radiance from their cars,
And fill'd the earth, from his deep throne,
With lonely lustre, all his own.

'Up rose the sun; the mists were curl'd
Back from the solitary world
Which lay around – behind – before:
What booted it to traverse o'er
Plain, forest, river? Man nor brute,
Nor dint of hoof, nor print of foot,
Lay in the wild luxuriant soil;
No sign of travel – none of toil;
The very air was mute;
And not an insect's shrill small horn,
Nor matin bird's new voice was borne
From herb nor thicket. Many a werst,
Panting as if his heart would burst,
The weary brute still stagger'd on;
And still we were – or seem'd – alone:

At length, while reeling on our way,
Methought I heard a courser neigh,
From out yon tuft of blackening firs.
Is it the wind those branches stirs?
No, no! from out the forest prance
    A trampling troop; I see them come!
In one vast squadron they advance!
    I strove to cry – my lips were dumb.
The steeds rush on in plunging pride;
But where are they the reins to guide?
A thousand horse – and none to ride!
With flowing tail, and flying mane,
Wide nostrils – never stretch'd by pain,
Mouths bloodless to the bit or rein,
And feet that iron never shod,
And flanks unscarr'd by spur or rod,
A thousand horse, the wild, the free,
Like waves that follow o'er the sea,
    Came thickly thundering on,
As if our faint approach to meet;
The sight re-nerved my courser's feet,
A moment staggering, feebly fleet,
A moment, with a faint low neigh,
    He answer'd, and then fell;
With gasps and glazing eyes he lay,
    And reeking limbs immoveable,
      His first and last career is done!
On came the troop – they saw him stoop,
    They saw me strangely bound along
    His back with many a bloody thong:
They stop – they start – they snuff the air,
Gallop a moment here and there,

Approach, retire, wheel round and round,
Then plunging back with sudden bound,
Headed by one black mighty steed,
Who seem'd the patriarch of his breed,
        Without a single speck or hair
Of white upon his shaggy hide;
They snort — they foam — neigh — swerve aside,
And backward to the forest fly,
By instinct, from a human eye. —
        They left me there to my despair,
Link'd to the dead and stiffening wretch,
Whose lifeless limbs beneath me stretch,
Relieved from that unwonted weight,
From whence I could not extricate
Nor him nor me — and there we lay
        The dying on the dead!
I little deem'd another day
        Would see my houseless, helpless head.
And there from morn till twilight bound,
I felt the heavy hours toil round,
With just enough of life to see
My last of suns go down on me.
And there from morn till twilight bound,
I felt the heavy hours toll round,
With just enough of life to see
My last of suns go down on me,
In hopeless certainty of mind,
That makes us feel at length resigned
To that which our foreboding years
Presents the worst and last of fears
Inevitable — even a boon,
Nor more unkind for coming soon,

Yet shunned and dreaded with such care,
As if it only were a snare
            That prudence might escape:
At times both wished for and implored,
At times sought with self-pointed sword,
Yet still a dark and hideous close
To even intolerable woes,
            And welcome in no shape.
And, strange to say, the sons of pleasure,
They who have revelled beyond measure
In beauty, wassail, wine, and treasure,
Die calm, or calmer, oft than he
Whose heritage was misery.
For he who hath in turn run through
All that was beautiful and new,
            Hath nought to hope, and nought to leave;
And, save the future, (which is viewed
Not quite as men are base or good,
But as their nerves may be endued,)
With nought perhaps to grieve:
The wretch still hopes his woes must end,
And death, whom he should deem his friend,
Appears, to his distempered eyes,
Arrived to rob him of his prize,
The tree of his new Paradise.
Tomorrow would have given him all,
Repaid his pangs, repaired his fall;
Tomorrow would have been the first
Of days no more deplored or curst,
But bright, and long, and beckoning years,
Seen dazzling through the mist of tears,
Guerdon of many a painful hour;

Tomorrow would have given him power
To rule, to shine, to smite, to save -
And must it dawn upon his grave?

'The sun was sinking - still I lay
Chained to the chill and stiffening steed,
I thought to mingle there our clay;
And my dim eyes of death had need,
No hope arose of being freed.
I cast my last looks up the sky,
And there between me and the sun
I saw the expecting raven fly,
Who scarce would wait till both should die,
Ere his repast begun;
He flew, and perched, then flew once more,
And each time nearer than before;
I saw his wing through twilight flit,
And once so near me he alit
I could have smote, but lacked the strength;
But the slight motion of my hand,
And feeble scratching of the sand,
The exerted throat's faint struggling noise,
Which scarcely could be called a voice,
I know no more – my latest dream
        Is something of a lovely star
        Which fix'd my dull eyes from afar,
And went and came with wandering beam,
And of the cold, dull, swimming, dense
Sensation of recurring sense,
And then subsiding back to death,
And then again a little breath,
A little thrill, a short suspense,

An icy sickness curdling o'er
My heart, and sparks that cross'd my brain –
A gasp, a throb, a start of pain,
    A sigh, and nothing more.

'I woke – Where was I? – Do I see
A human face look down on me?
And doth a roof above me close?
Do these limbs on a couch repose?
Is this a chamber where I lie?
And is it mortal yon bright eye,
That watches me with gentle glance?
    I closed my own again once more,
As doubtful that the former trance
    Could not as yet be o'er.
A slender girl, long-hair'd, and tall,
Sate watching by the cottage wall;
The sparkle of her eye I caught,
Even with my first return of thought;
For ever and anon she threw
    A prying, pitying glance on me
    With her black eyes so wild and free:
I gazed, and gazed, until I knew
    No vision it could be, –
But that I lived, and was released
From adding to the vulture's feast:
And when the Cossack maid beheld
My heavy eyes at length unseal'd,
She smiled – and I essay'd to speak,
    But fail'd – and she approach'd, and made
    With lip and finger signs that said,
I must not strive as yet to break

The silence, till my strength should be
Enough to leave my accents free;
And then her hand on mine she laid,
And smooth'd the pillow for my head,
And stole along on tiptoe tread,
     And gently oped the door, and spake
In whispers — ne'er was voice so sweet!
Even music follow'd her light feet; —
     But those she call'd were not awake,
And she went forth; but, ere she pass'd,
Another look on me she cast,
     Another sign she made, to say,
That I had nought to fear, that all
Were near, at my command or call,
     And she would not delay
Her due return: — while she was gone,
Methought I felt too much alone.

She came with mother and with sire —
What need of more? — I will not tire
With long recital of the rest,
Since I became the Cossack's guest.
They found me senseless on the plain —
     They bore me to the nearest hut —
They brought me into life again —
Me — one day o'er their realm to reign!

Poetic Commandments (from *Don Juan*, Canto I)

If ever I should condescend to prose,
    I'll write poetical commandments, which
Shall supersede beyond all doubt all those
    That went before; in these I shall enrich
My text with many things that no one knows,
    And carry precept to the highest pitch:
I'll call the work 'Longinus o'er a Bottle,
Or, Every Poet his own Aristotle'.

Thou shalt believe in Milton, Dryden, Pope;
    Thou shalt not set up Wordsworth, Coleridge,
      Southey;
Because the first is crazed beyond all hope,
    The second drunk, the third so quaint and mouthey:
With Crabbe it may be difficult to cope,
    And Campbell's Hipprocrene is somewhat drouthy:
Thou shalt not steal from Samuel Rogers, nor
Commit – flirtation with the muse of Moore.

Thou shalt not covet Mr Sotheby's Muse,
    His Pegasus, nor any thing that's his;
Thou shalt not bear false witness like 'the Blues',
    (There's one, at least, is very fond of this);
Thou shalt not write, in short, but what I choose:
    This is true criticism, and you may kiss –
Exactly as you please, or not, the rod,
But if you don't, I'll lay it on, by G—d!

Stanzas to the Po

I

River, that rollest by the ancient walls,
 Where dwells the Lady of my love, when she
Walks by thy brink, and there perchance recalls
 A faint and fleeting memory of me:

II

What if thy deep and ample stream should be
 A mirror of my heart, where she may read
The thousand thoughts I now betray to thee,
 Wild as thy wave, and headlong as thy speed!

III

What do I say — a mirror of my heart?
 Are not thy waters sweeping, dark, and strong?
Such as my feelings were and are, thou art;
 And such as thou art were my passions long.

IV

Time may have somewhat tamed them, — not for ever;
 Thou overflow'st thy banks, and not for aye
Thy bosom overboils, congenial river!
 Thy floods subside, and mine have sunk away:

V

But left long wrecks behind, and now again,
 Borne in our old unchanged career, we move:
Thou tendest wildly onwards to the main,
 And I — to loving one I should not love.

VI

The current I behold will sweep beneath
    Her native walls, and murmur at her feet;
Her eyes will look on thee, when she shall breathe
    The twilight air, unharmed by summer's heat.

VII

She will look on thee, — I have looked on thee,
    Full of that thought: and, from that moment,
      ne'er
Thy waters could I dream of, name, or see,
    Without the inseparable sigh for her!

VIII

Her bright eyes will be imaged in thy stream, —
    Yes! they will meet the wave I gaze on now:
Mine cannot witness, even in a dream,
    That happy wave repass me in its flow!

IX

The wave that bears my tears returns no more:
    Will she return by whom that wave shall sweep? —
Both tread thy banks, both wander on thy shore,
    I by thy source, she by the dark-blue deep.

X

But that which keepeth us apart is not
    Distance, nor depth of wave, nor space of earth,
But the distraction of a various lot,
    As various as the climates of our birth.

XI

A stranger loves the Lady of the land,
    Born far beyond the mountains, but his blood
Is all meridian, as if never fanned
    By the black wind that chills the polar flood.

XII

My blood is all meridian; were it not,
    I had not left my clime, nor should I be,
In spite of tortures, ne'er to be forgot,
    A slave again of love, – at least of thee.

XIII

'Tis vain to struggle – let me perish young –
    Live as I lived, and love as I have loved;
To dust if I return, from dust I sprung,
    And then, at least, my heart can ne'er be moved.

Evening (from *Don Juan*, Canto III)

Ave Maria! o'er the earth and sea,
That heavenliest hour of heaven is worthiest thee!

Ave Maria! blessed be the hour,
    The time, the clime, the spot, where I so oft
Have felt that moment in its fullest power
    Sink o'er the earth so beautiful and soft,
While swung the deep bell in the distant tower,
    Or the faint dying day-hymn stole aloft,
And not a breath crept through the rosy air,
And yet the forest leaves seemed stirred with prayer.

Ave Maria! 'tis the hour of prayer!
    Ave Maria! 'tis the hour of love!
Ave Maria! may our spirits dare
    Look up to thine and to thy Son's above!
Ave Maria! O that face so fair!
    Those downcast eyes beneath the Almighty dove –
What though 'tis but a pictured image? – strike –
That painting is no idol, – 'tis too like.

Some kinder casuists are pleased to say,
    In nameless print – that I have no devotion;
But set those persons down with me to pray,
    And you shall see who has the properest notion
Of getting into Heaven the shortest way;
    My altars are the mountains and the ocean,
Earth, air, stars, – all that springs from the great Whole,
Who hath produced, and will receive the soul.

Sweet hour of twilight! in the solitude
    Of the pine forest, and the silent shore
Which bounds Ravenna's immemorial wood,
    Rooted where once the Adrian wave flowed o'er
To where the last Cæsarean fortress stood,
    Evergreen forest! which Boccaccio's lore
And Dryden's lay made haunted ground to me,
How have I loved the twilight hour and thee!

The shrill cicalas, people of the pine,
    Making their summer lives one ceaseless song,
Were the sole echoes, save my steed's and mine,
    And vesper bells that rose the boughs along;
The spectre huntsman of Onesti's line,
    His hell-dogs, and their chase, and the fair throng
Which learned from this example not to fly
From a true lover, – shadowed my mind's eye.

O Hesperus! thou bringest all good things –
    Home to the weary, to the hungry cheer,
To the young bird the parent's brooding wings,
    The welcome stall to the o'erlaboured steer;
Whate'er of peace about our hearthstone clings,
    Whate'er our household gods protect of dear,
Are gathered round us by thy look of rest;
Thou bring'st the child, too, to the mother's breast.

Soft hour! which wakes the wish and melts the heart
    Of those who sail the seas, on the first day
When they from their sweet friends are torn apart;
    Or fills with love the pilgrim on his way
As the far bell of vesper makes him start,

Seeming to weep the dying day's decay;
Is this a fancy which our reason scorns?
Ah! surely nothing dies but something mourns!

The Isles of Greece (from *Don Juan*, Canto III)

I

The isles of Greece, the Isles of Greece!
　　Where burning Sappho loved and sung,
Where grew the arts of war and peace,
　　Where Delos rose, and Phoebus sprung!
Eternal summer gilds them yet,
But all, except their sun, is set.

II

The Scian and the Teian muse,
　　The hero's harp, the lover's lute,
Have found the fame your shores refuse;
　　Their place of birth alone is mute
To sounds which echo further west
　　Than your sires' 'Islands of the Blest'.

III

The mountains look on Marathon –
　　And Marathon looks on the sea;
And musing there an hour alone,
　　I dream'd that Greece might still be free;
For standing on the Persians' grave,
I could not deem myself a slave.

IV

A king sate on the rocky brow
　　Which looks o'er sea-born Salamis;
And ships, by thousands, lay below,
　　And men in nations; – all were his!

He counted them at break of day —
And when the sun set where were they?

V

And where are they? and where art thou,
     My country? On thy voiceless shore
The heroic lay is tuneless now —
     The heroic bosom beats no more!
And must thy lyre, so long divine,
Degenerate into hands like mine?

VI

'Tis something, in the dearth of fame,
     Though link'd among a fetter'd race,
To feel at least a patriot's shame,
     Even as I sing, suffuse my face;
For what is left the poet here?
For Greeks a blush — for Greece a tear.

VII

Must *we* but weep o'er days more blest?
     Must *we* but blush? — Our fathers bled.
Earth! render back from out thy breast
     A remnant of our Spartan dead!
Of the three hundred grant but three,
To make a new Thermopylae!

VIII

What, silent still? and silent all?
     Ah! no; — the voices of the dead
Sound like a distant torrent's fall,
     And answer, 'Let one living head,

But one arise, – we come, we come!'
'Tis but the living who are dumb.

IX

In vain – in vain: strike other chords;
 Fill high the cup with Samian wine!
Leave battles to the Turkish hordes,
 And shed the blood of Scio's vine!
Hark! rising to the ignoble call –
How answers each bold Bacchanal!

X

You have the Pyrrhic dance as yet,
 Where is the Pyrrhic phalanx gone?
Of two such lessons, why forget
 The nobler and the manlier one?
You have the letters Cadmus gave –
Think ye he meant them for a slave?

XI

Fill high the bowl with Samian wine!
 We will not think of themes like these!
It made Anacreon's song divine:
 He served – but served Polycrates –
A tyrant; but our masters then
Were still, at least, our countrymen.

XII

The tyrant of the Chersonese
 Was freedom's best and bravest friend;
That tyrant was Miltiades!
Oh! that the present hour would lend

Another despot of the kind!
Such chains as his were sure to bind.

XIII

Fill high the bowl with Samian wine!
 On Suli's rock, and Parga's shore,
Exists the remnant of a line
 Such as the Doric mothers bore;
And there, perhaps, some seed is sown,
The Heracleidan blood might own.

XIV

Trust not for freedom to the Franks –
 They have a king who buys and sells;
In native swords, and native ranks,
 The only hope of courage dwells;
But Turkish force, and Latin fraud,
Would break your shield, however broad.

XV

Fill high the bowl with Samian wine!
 Our virgins dance beneath the shade –
I see their glorious black eyes shine;
 But gazing on each glowing maid,
My own the burning tear-drop laves,
To think such breasts must suckle slaves.

XVI

Place me on Sunium's marbled steep,
 Where nothing, save the waves and I,
May hear our mutual murmurs sweep;
 There, swan-like, let me sing and die:

A land of slaves shall ne'er be mine —
Dash down yon cup of Samian wine!

John Keats

Who killed John Keats?
'I,' says the Quarterly,
So savage and Tartarly;
''Twas one of my feats.'

Who shot the arrow?
'The poet-priest Milman
(So ready to kill man),
Or Southey or Barrow.'

When a Man Hath No Freedom to Fight for at Home

When a man hath no freedom to fight for at home,
    Let him combat for that of his neighbours;
Let him think of the glories of Greece and of Rome,
    And get knocked on the head for his labours.

To do good to Mankind is the chivalrous plan,
    And is always as nobly requited;
Then battle for Freedom wherever you can,
    And, if not shot or hanged, you'll get knighted.

Stanzas Written on the Road Between Florence and Pisa

Oh, talk not to me of a name great in story;
The days of our youth are the days of our glory;
And the myrtle and ivy of sweet two-and-twenty
Are worth all your laurels, though ever so plenty.

What are garlands and crowns to the brow that is
   wrinkled?
'Tis but as a dead flower with May-dew besprinkled.
Then away with all such from the head that is hoary!
What care I for the wreaths that can only give glory!

Oh FAME! – if I e'er took delight in thy praises,
'Twas less for the sake of thy high-sounding phrases,
Than to see the bright eyes of the dear one discover,
She thought that I was not unworthy to love her.

There chiefly I sought thee, there only I found thee;
Her glance was the best of the rays that surround thee;
When it sparkled o'er aught that was bright in my story,
I knew it was love, and I felt it was glory.

Invocation to the Spirit of Achilles (from *The Deformed Transformed*)

Beautiful shadow
    Of Thetis's boy!
Who sleeps in the meadow
    Whose grass grows o'er Troy:
From the red earth, like Adam,
    Thy likeness I shape,
As the being who made him,
    Whose actions I ape.
Thou clay, be all glowing,
    Till the rose in his cheek
Be as fair as, when blowing,
    It wears its first streak!
Ye violets, I scatter,
    Now turn into eyes!
And thou, sunshiny water,
    Of blood take the guise!
Let these hyacinth boughs
    Be his long flowing hair,
And wave o'er his brows
    As thou wavest in air!
Let his heart be this marble
    I tear from the rock!
But his voice as the warble
    Of birds on yon oak!
Let his flesh be the purest
    Of mould, in which grew
The lily-root surest,
    And drank the best dew!
Let his limbs be the lightest

Which clay can compound,
And his aspect the brightest
    On earth to be found!
Elements, near me,
    Be mingled and stirr'd,
Know me, and hear me,
    And leap to my word!
Sunbeams, awaken
    This earth's animation!
'Tis done! He hath taken
    His stand in creation!

On This Day I Complete My Thirty-Sixth Year

I

'Tis time this heart should be unmoved,
    Since others it hath ceased to move:
Yet, though I cannot be beloved,
      Still let me love!

II

My days are in the yellow leaf;
    The flowers and fruits of Love are gone;
The worm, the canker, and the grief
      Are mine alone!

III

The fire that on my bosom preys
    Is lone as some Volcanic Isle;
No torch is kindled at its blaze —
      A funeral pile.

IV

The hope, the fear, the jealous care,
    The exalted portion of the pain
And power of Love, I cannot share,
      But wear the chain.

V

But 'tis not thus — and 'tis not here —
    Such thoughts should shake my Soul, nor now
Where Glory decks the hero's bier,
      Or binds his brow.

VI

The Sword, the Banner, and the Field,
  Glory and Greece, around me see!
The Spartan, borne upon his shield,
   Was not more free.

VII

Awake! (not Greece – she *is* awake!)
  Awake, my spirit! Think through *whom*
Thy life-blood tracks its parent lake,
   And then strike home!

VIII

Tread those reviving passions down,
  Unworthy Manhood! – unto thee
Indifferent should the smile or frown
   Of Beauty be.

IX

If thou regret'st thy youth, *why live?*
  The land of honourable Death
Is here: – up to the Field, and give
   Away thy Breath!

X

Seek out – less often sought than found –
  A Soldier's Grave, for thee the best;
Then look around, and choose thy Ground,
   And take thy Rest.

Love and Death

I watched thee when the foe was at our side,
Ready to strike at him — or thee and me,
Were safety hopeless — rather than divide
Aught with one loved save love and liberty.

I watched thee on the breakers, when the rock,
Received our prow, and all was storm and fear,
And bade thee cling to me through every shock;
This arm would be thy bark, or breast thy bier.

I watched thee when the fever glazed thine eyes,
Yielding my couch and stretched me on the ground
When overworn with watching, ne'er to rise
From thence if thou an early grave hadst found.

The earthquake came, and rocked the quivering wall,
And men and nature reeled as if with wine.
Whom did I seek around the tottering hall?
For thee. Whose safety first provide for? Thine.

And when convulsive throes denied my breath
The faintest utterance to my fading thought,
To thee — to thee — e'en in the gasp of death
My spirit turned, oh! oftener than it ought.

Thus much and more; and yet thou lov'st me not,
And never wilt! Love dwells not in our will.
Nor can I blame thee, though it be my lot
To strongly, wrongly, vainly love thee still.

Index of First Lines